Ausiled Teacher Scheme

D0316164

Topic Work in the Early Years

For more than twenty years, topic work has been accepted as the 'natural' way to teach young children in their first years of school. The introduction of a subject-based curriculum in England and Wales has led to intense questioning of that assured position. Teachers and others are wondering whether the topic approach can fulfil the requirements of the National Curriculum and whether in any case it is necessarily the best way of teaching young children.

The authors of *Topic Work in the Early Years* argue that the answer is 'yes' in both cases although neither this nor any other strategy should be used exclusively in the classroom. With the help of detailed case studies, they give guidance on the planning and assessment of topic work within and across subjects and show how topics can be planned to fulfil specific curricular requirements while retaining the particular virtues of the topic approach: flexibility in the use of time and resources, the chance for coverage of certain areas in greater depth and differentiation of tasks among children at various stages of their development. Individual chapters cover planning and assessment of topic work across the curriculum, cross-curricular issues and topic work in the core subjects of the National Curriculum as well as history and geography.

Joy Palmer is Senior Lecturer in Education at the University of Durham. She is a former primary school teacher and head of a primary centre and has published extensively in the areas of primary curriculum and environmental education. She is the series editor for the Routledge series *Teaching and Learning in the First Three Years of School*. **Deirdre Pettitt** taught for some years in infant schools and is now Lecturer in Education at the University of Durham. Her publications include *Beginning Writing* (1989).

Topic Work
in the Early Years

Organising the curriculum
for 4- to 8-year-olds

Joy Palmer and Deirdre Pettitt

London and New York

First published 1993
by Routledge
11 New Fetter Lane, London EC4P 4EE

Simultaneously published in the USA and Canada
by Routledge
29 West 35th Street, New York, NY 10001

Typeset in Palatino by LaserScript, Mitcham, Surrey
Printed and bound in Great Britain by
Mackays of Chatham PLC, Chatham, Kent

British Library Cataloguing in Publication Data
A catalogue record for this book is available from the British Library

Library of Congress Cataloging in Publication Data
has been applied for.

ISBN 0–415–08041–x

Contents

Illustrations

FIGURES

TABLE

Preface

We do not expect nor would we want everyone who is involved in educating young children to agree with our ideas. We have tried to argue our case coherently drawing on our experience and making our own interpretation of the available evidence. If some readers reject what we say we have no quarrel with that. However, we shall be disappointed if we have not been able to raise questions about topic work in all our readers' minds. Uncertainty is a constant feature in teaching at any level as good teachers question their own philosophy, practice and performance. This professional uncertainty must be as well informed as possible. Some would argue that outside the classroom, teachers have not been very good at explaining what they do and why they do it. Perhaps there is an urgent need to get better at this in the face of certainty about education from many sources, which is grossly uninformed.

Chapter 1

Topic work in the early years
Introduction

This book arises out of our own experience of teaching young children, our work with students in teacher education and our in-service work with teachers. All these experiences have led us to the conclusion that topic work has and should continue to have an important role to play in the curriculum for young children. We wish to share with our readers our reasons for coming to this conclusion. Topic work is widely used. This book attempts to justify and exemplify its use.

The framework within which schools and teachers implement the curriculum is shaped by the statutory provisions contained in the various National Curriculum documents. How, and to a more limited extent when, the knowledge, skills and understandings of the core and foundation subjects, religious education and cross-curricular themes are translated into schemes of work was left to teachers. In the 1990s the government, anxious to see success for its reforms, may move more and more towards control of methods of implementing the curriculum. An early indication of this trend was the commissioning of the discussion paper entitled 'Curriculum Organisation and Classroom Practice in Primary Schools' (Alexander *et al.* 1992). The implications of this discussion paper were that teachers must be able to justify their practices, including topic work. The discussion paper stated

> If it can be shown that the topic approach allows the pupil both to make acceptable progress within the different subjects of the National Curriculum and to explore the relationships between them, then the case for such an approach is strong on both pedagogic and logistical grounds. If however, the result is that the difference between subjects is extinguished the strategy is indefensible.
>
> (Alexander *et al.* 1992)

The paper went on to criticise topic work which is undemanding, wastes children's time, does not make full use of the National Curriculum programmes of study and which limits such subjects as art, history and geography. It did not deny that 'the topic approach in skilled hands can produce work of good quality' (ibid.) and praised the move from 'divergent' topics with considerable choice to 'broad-based' topics and 'subject-focused' topics. (The former are where a theme such as transport 'is used to bring together content and skills from several subjects' (ibid.) and the latter 'where pupils concentrate on a limited number of attainment targets from other subjects' (ibid.)) Subject-focused topics are preferred in the discussion paper because 'they can be planned more easily in relation to the standing orders and can provide more appropriately for the sequential development of pupils' knowledge understanding and skills' (ibid.).

In respect of this preference for subject-based topics, it can be argued that there are times when broad-based topics could be seen as more important to children's learning and to the development of the subject(s) being taught. At other times, subject-focused topics might be more appropriate. In making this judgement the difficulty of planning to meet statutory orders ought not to be an excuse for abandoning broad-based topics. In this book, examples of both sorts of topics will be advanced although in some cases the distinction will not be clear cut.

The discussion paper referred to the whole primary curriculum and was intended to be a forum for discussion for everyone concerned with that curriculum. Primary schooling in England and Wales is organised in various ways to accommodate children between the ages of 5 and 11. Parents are not required to send children of 4 years old to school but many do so even where there is good nursery provision. (In that case children frequently attend nursery but are sent to school at 4.) There are many terms which are used to identify different age groups of children and these differ between countries. It has been decided, in this book, to use the term 'early years' to refer to children aged between 4 and 8 years old who are in school. In the discussion paper some points were specific to older primary children, such as whether or not they should be taught by subject specialists. However, much else applied equally to younger and older children.

Having defined the age range to be discussed, it is necessary to ask to what extent suggestions which are put forward about topic work in the early years differ from those which might have been made for older children. The answer is not very much. There is a huge range of attainment and ability to be catered for in any primary classroom. As children get older the curriculum provides for higher levels of cognition and more extensive knowledge. However, at any age, the essential factor is the view of learning which pervades our thinking. Broadly, it is held that teaching for learning, however it is implemented, builds on existing knowledge and experience and the schemata which each learner has constructed in the mind. Given this view it may be that the principles we suggest for the curriculum including topic work obtain generally.

Although an age range has been demarcated for analysis, this view of learning (which will be elaborated on later) raises further questions about whether it is appropriate to make sharp divisions between children related to age, rather than experience and attainment. It is at least possible that the way schools have been organised has had some effect on references to 'the 4-year-old' or 'the 7-year-old'. Perhaps we should consider whether there is any such thing as a typical or normal child of any age. Of course this consideration raises enormous practical difficulties in schools. Selections of content and ways of organising knowledge must, in reality, be made to meet the strengths of the majority of children. Classes in the early years are frequently, but not invariably, age related. Within any class, levels of experience and attainment will differ not only between but also within curriculum areas. And this will also apply to affective, physical and social levels. Matching is a key issue for all teachers (Ausubel 1968, Bennett and Desforges 1988), and it may be that topic work facilitates this task.

This book makes suggestions about content which are mainly derived from the National Curriculum at Key Stage 1. (This is not a simple procedure for authors or teachers because it seems to change almost daily.) Nevertheless, while it is not intended to limit suggestions to the National Curriculum, no apologies are made for its use. This is what teachers must do and its aims are, perforce, theirs. As noted above, at least for the time being, much of how to implement the curriculum rather than what it should consist of is left to schools. We suggest that topic work is an opportunity for the exploration of subject matter in depth. Given the pressure for linear coverage in the curriculum, there may be a danger of sacrificing depth for quick movement up the levels of the National Curriculum, and topics may redress the balance. Teachers' aims will include appropriate depth. However, if topics themselves become too diffuse they may defeat the aim of giving children space and time to think, to ask questions, to use and apply their knowledge and to begin to take some control over their own learning. The paradox is that this aim may require that a topic has defined boundaries and does not seek to cover every area of the curriculum. Information overload may not just be a problem for teachers (Desforges and Cockburn 1987), it may also be a problem for children. Teachers who aim for understanding – which takes time to learn – may have to limit content to ensure that what is covered is covered thoroughly (Brophy 1989).

In the first chapter we elaborate on the infant teacher's task and set this in the context of the National Curriculum. We suggest how and why topic work can be used in this task to promote the learning of young children.

In subsequent chapters we turn to classroom practice in the use of topics and themes. Chapter 2 is about planning, assessment, evaluating and recording. Each of the following chapters takes a curriculum area as its focus and shows how a topic may be developed, taking account of teaching and learning processes and presenting case studies and examples. The curriculum areas selected to illustrate our ideas are English, mathematics, science, history, geography, and cross-curricular issues. The importance of other subjects in the National Curriculum and religious education is clear. Where these can arise in the topics we develop, they have been included. The selection made derives from specific expertise and is limited by space. In considering those subjects we have been able to cover in some depth, readers may be able to identify others which could be used as unifying elements in a topic. Throughout, we draw on many sources, but our debt to the practising teachers and students with whom we have worked is evident. We acknowledge this debt and their expertise, and in what follows our intention is not to prescribe but to suggest what we have learned and are still learning about young children thinking and learning in classrooms.

THE BACKGROUND ISSUES

The infant school and the teacher's task

We believe that teaching in the early years of schooling is both an intellectually and a physically demanding task. No one should ever underestimate what young children can do and the challenges they present to teachers. The first two or three years of formal schooling which children have is a period to which they bring widely differing experiences and levels of attainment. The combination of the wide ranging areas of experience to be taken into account, together with individual differences in ability and attainment, demands the total commitment of teachers, and we take their task very seriously indeed.

   Some of the aims of early years teaching are probably generally accepted. Teachers have always tried to implement a 'broad and balanced curriculum' which includes an introduction to knowledge valued by our society. Socially valued knowledge, as far as schooling from 5 to 16 is concerned, has been written in the National Curriculum under subject headings, and although the various non-statutory guidelines frequently point to the connections between subjects, it seems clear that each of the working parties engaged in advising on content was satisfied that its own discipline had distinctive knowledge claims, principles and ways of thinking. No one would deny that interesting discoveries are made on the margins between subjects and by applying models from one subject to illuminate another. Beyond schooling from 5 to 16, and indeed within it, subjects amalgamate or are narrowed down into many different sub-areas. However, the organisation of knowledge into the subjects of schooling from 5 to 16 seems at least as reasonable as any other. Moreover, it is possible that the subjects selected, which have evolved over time as those considered appropriate for school, have done so because they reflect the culture of the day (i.e. they differ from the elementary curriculum of relatively recent years and certainly look very different from that studied by Shakespeare). In this culture, school subjects as they are presently conceived seem to be a reflection of what is useful and interesting to the population.

A relevant question may be to ask whether knowledge should be organised differently for young children. It might be surmised that young children are also interested in knowledge which their culture embodies. Other ways of organising knowledge have, however, been recommended for the primary school. For example, in 1989 Her Majesty's Inspectorate (HMI) identified content categories: human and social, linguistic and literary, mathematical, moral, physical, scientific, spiritual and technological (DES 1989c). They added further lists of concepts, skills and attitudes derived from these categories. Without disputing the value of any of these categories, they do seem, however, to be more limited than the present curriculum and to derive from a subject basis. It may, therefore be sensible to retain the organisation of knowledge into subjects as a starting point for the organisation of the curriculum, quite apart from the fact that the National Curriculum has done precisely this. As has been pointed out: 'Subjects, as conventionally defined, are the major component of even the most espousedly undifferentiated curriculum' (Alexander 1984).

Organising knowledge in the curriculum directly from children's interests might be ideal, given the skill to guide such interests, whether we like it or not, towards the attainment targets of the National Curriculum. In practice (a) the interests of a class of children will vary, (b) the sheer size of classes poses enormous difficulties, and (c) it may be that teachers' skills should be employed to widen children's horizons and engender interests rather than follow them. These points and our acceptance of knowledge organised by subjects are not antithetical to a child-centred approach. There is no necessary conflict between subjects and the existing knowledge and experience of the child, any more than there is between the latter and *ad hoc* categories of human experience.

Finally, the empirical view of knowledge coherently and fully argued in, for example, Blenkin and Kelly (1987) must be acknowledged. This view, which cannot be dealt with adequately here, contains a defence of a skills-based, process-oriented curriculum. Within this large corpus of work we find the best of progressive education summarised as:

> the attempt to treat a child as a child, the emphasis on education through experience and learning by discovery, the view of knowledge as integrated or at least not compartmentalised, the attention to developmental stages and the definition of education and curriculum in terms of processes.
>
> (Blenkin and Kelly 1987)

Some of this is incontestable. However 'developmental stages' are at least problematic (Donaldson 1978) and may be seen as defined by contexts. More important perhaps, is that the difficulty of implementing a curriculum on this basis is such that its ideals seem rarely to be implemented in practice (Alexander 1984, Desforges and Cockburn 1987). In our view, however, the following criticism carries most weight:

> [I]t is evident that some drastic decisions have to be made about curriculum priorities in the light of judgements about what it is reasonable to attain rather than dreams about what is desirable. In addressing this problem some experts (for example Blenkin and Kelly 1983) have suggested the adoption of a process curriculum. In brief, this entails the identification of significant learning and thinking processes with which we wish children to engage. A curriculum is then built around the design of opportunities to acquire and exercise such intellectual facilities.
>
> There are problems with this approach, not least of which are (a) there is lack of agreement on whether it is sensible to conceive of learning processes independent of content; (b) there is lack of agreement on what such processes might be; and lists of skills can run to thousands of elements. In short the idea might not provide the economies of time necessary to putting it into practice even if the general model were tenable.
>
> (Desforges and Cockburn 1987)

Item (a) seems a little unfair. Content is not seen as unimportant in a unified curriculum, but to some extent knowledge is seen as more important than processes.

Having looked, necessarily rather briefly, at different ways of organising knowledge and therefore of organising the curriculum, we have come down on the side of using subjects as a basis. In our detailed descriptions of how this might work and at the same time retain children at the centre, we try to show that the aims of teachers to implement a 'broad and balanced curriculum' need not abandon progressive ideals of the best sort.

In addition to cognitive content, teachers include in their aims the social, emotional and moral development of children. As well as being important in their own right, these are inextricably interwoven with the attainment of knowledge, skills and understandings of the more formal sort. Perhaps at any age relationships with teachers and peers are crucial, but early years teachers know that it is unlikely that young children can learn easily without confidence in their teachers and a secure environment. Teachers are both role model and guide. They must accept children as they are but present standards and values children can follow without denigrating the standards and values they bring to school.

Teachers in the early years of school also aim to ensure that children enjoy their activities and learn how to learn. Children are helped to develop a self-image that is positive enough to accept criticism, to be self-critical, to be curious and to feel free to make mistakes and learn from them.

The attainment of what are generally known as the basic skills, usually of literacy and numeracy, is a further aim. Learning basic skills is part of the entitlement of all children. All children need and can achieve competencies which they must have to enable them to make choices in their lives. It seems at least possible that failing to learn to read and write in the early years for example, is difficult to remedy later. A good start lays the foundations on which colleagues can build.

The advent of the National Curriculum has not altered the task of teachers, although it has extended it and is now the framework in which it must be accomplished. In particular, increased attention to the foundations of socially valued knowledge has to be accommodated in the curriculum, whatever method is employed.

The National Curriculum

Since 1989 infant schools in England and Wales have been required to implement the National Curriculum. One effect, as we pointed out earlier is that the breadth of the curriculum has been widened. Teachers are required to incorporate the core subjects (mathematics, English and science), the foundation subjects (history, geography, technology (including design), music, art and physical education) and religious education, to form the basic curriculum. Within and alongside these subjects the cross-curricular themes – economic and industrial understanding, careers education and guidance, health education, education for citizenship and environmental education – must be attended to, where appropriate, together with personal and social education. Of course much of this was already the staple diet of the early years curriculum, but most schools have probably had to rethink some of the curriculum to include some new dimensions and extend others. This has necessitated a careful examination of how time is used in a classroom. Studies have indicated that a good deal of the infant day can be used unproductively (Tizard *et al.* 1988) and clearly planning a 'broad and balanced curriculum' must attend to this problem. Equally, schools have had to 'seek to identify the considerable overlaps which inevitably exist in both content and skills' (NCC 1990).

This new breadth in the curriculum is to be welcomed as it indicates faith in the ability of young children to learn across a range of activities which traditionally were thought to be beyond their capabilities. Implementing the National Curriculum also demands that teachers' schemes of work, derived from the programmes of study, attend to the processes involved in learning at each level. The National Curriculum could be thought of as wholly product oriented. It could become so if the attainment targets were the only determinant of the curriculum and the processes of learning and variety of experience were not included. The attainment targets are goals or aims which are the end product. The route to the end product can incorporate the wider aims of the teachers.

At Key Stage 1 the National Curriculum documents and the *Non-Statutory Guidance* stress the importance of the foundations of knowledge, skills and understandings being laid in each subject. In order that this can be done, the documents invariably stress the range of different experiences which children will need in order to begin to understand these foundations. For example, attainment target 1 of Mathematics 5–16 relates to the use and application of mathematics (DES 1991a). This confirms the view of teachers that one way of developing understanding is the use of knowledge and skills in different situations. Children make sense of what they have learned when they apply it, especially in a new context. The major thrust of the Cockroft Report (Cockroft 1982) was that although children could do basic mathematical routines, typically, they were unable to transfer what they had learned in these procedural tasks to applications in other, often more everyday, situations. The National Curriculum in mathematics owes much to Cockroft but more generally this emphasis on uses of knowledge and skills and broad experience is reiterated across the curriculum specified for all subjects.

Progression and continuity in the National Curriculum

It is expected that children should progress in their learning. This is no simple matter. We may be looking for the attainment of new skills, for a simple progression like moving from being able to count to five to being able to count to ten, or for a complex progression involving the grasp of abstract principles such as the nature of evidence or transfer of existing knowledge to new situations. Progression is looked for in the individual child and is evidenced by differences in his or her behaviour. In the National Curriculum, assessment of progression attempts to cover the full range of progress that children will make between the ages of 5 and 16. Levels of achievement have been identified in profile components and numbered from 1 to 10, but it is important to remember that these levels are not age related. That is, for example, level 1 is the first level to be attained no matter what the age of the child.

The whole notion of levels can be productive. Children are entitled to receive the whole curriculum up to and including the top level they are capable of reaching. We feel this could go some way to preventing both the underestimation of the more able and the abandonment of the less able. In the early years, the latter, in particular, have sometimes spent too long on what they cannot yet do, often limited by not being able to read and write very well, and not enough time on broader aspects of the curriculum to which they can contribute in other ways, for example, by displaying their general knowledge or attainments orally. Other ways of contributing and learning might well enable them to shine for once, and success can spin off productively. At the same time, the more able can be challenged. Identifying teaching strategies so as to promote progression demands that teachers develop diagnostic skills in order to ascertain where children are in their learning and plan their next moves. In the National Curriculum these diagnostic skills will be deployed both on a day-to-day basis and for the stipulated teacher assessments which take place for reporting purposes (at age 7 for Key Stage 1).

Progression has to relate to the planned curriculum manifested in school policies and overall schemes of work. The planned curriculum also provides for continuity and coherence within a school and between schools. One of the acknowledged benefits of the National Curriculum is the prospect of avoiding discontinuity of experience within schools and across schools because of the common curriculum and the extensive assessment and recording required of teachers. Planning for the early years classroom requires consideration of what may have been done in the nursery and what will be done in Key Stage 2. The National Curri- culum provides a common core but this will not ensure continuity or progression unless there is real communication at a detailed level between phases and, of course, between teachers in the same school.

TOPIC WORK

The teacher's task within the National Curriculum is to decide how best to plan and implement the content specified and frequently to go beyond this to retain broader aims. One definition of the task has been made:

> In the National Curriculum reports there is an explicit recognition that if children are to learn they must be engaged in 'brains on' activity. Intellectual processes must be operated. If teachers are to be effective they must have a powerful grasp of the subject matter they presume to teach. Equally they must understand children's intellectual processes and how and when best to teach them.
>
> (Desforges 1989)

This definition and our description of the teacher's task sets out what has to be done. Schools and teachers have to decide how they will do it. It is a traditional and accepted way of working in the early years classroom that a substantial part of the curriculum can be accomplished effectively by topic work. We agree, but maintain that to be effective and justifiable topic work must come under critical scrutiny. We must be able to defend the use of topics on current educational grounds and it is our purpose to do this. In the first instance it is necessary to look at what topic work is.

What is meant by topic work?

There are many interpretations of what a topic looks like and how it can be implemented. Broadly, a topic could be defined as a programme of work for children which is planned to occur over a variable period of time, depending on its content and the age and aptitudes of the children. It is a style of organising experience which can be contrasted with others such as play, instruction in skills and knowledge, or focus on skills and processes, not because it excludes these but because it includes them as appropriate. It is expected that children will be able to pursue the knowledge, skills and understandings embodied in the topic to some depth.

Traditionally and profitably, a topic in the early years classroom is multisensory. That is, it includes opportunities for children to use all their senses (to hear, see, touch, handle, smell, taste) and to apply these experiences to organise their thinking and extend their knowledge. A topic also enables them to learn, practise and apply skills such as reading, writing, drawing, speaking, listening, measuring, observing and classifying in context.

A topic normally has a unifying theme which unites the various elements within it. Teachers can identify the content of these elements with reference to National Curriculum subjects and issues. The importance of a topic based approach is that the content can be acquired in a context which makes sense to children; that is, they can identify purposes for their endeavours. Of course, children could engage in reading, writing, painting, investigating, solving problems in short all the multifarious activities which enable them to learn without doing topics at all. However, a topic can be a rich source of activities for which children can see a purpose. For example, it may make more sense to children to write about the weather in a topic on winter as a result of their observations, than to write 'The sun is sh . . . . . today' as a word filling exercise (especially when it is raining). Her Majesty's Inspectorate pointed out as long ago as 1978 (DES 1978) that there is no evidence to show that a concentration on the basic skills in isolation is the best way to teach them. Currently, research in the United States is beginning to provide evidence that isolated skill practice, for example in mathematics, is less productive than a programme where children engage in oral exploration of word problems with the teacher (Fennema *et al.* 1989).

A topic, then, will include opportunities for the practice of basic skills, but in a broad framework. Children will not only learn about the subject matter by reading and writing about it, for example, but they will also learn how to read and write for different purposes and in different genres. A topic, however, cannot be justified on those grounds alone. There are other criteria which are necessary, particularly in respect of content. We have suggested that a topic should have a unifying theme, but we need to consider what such a theme should embody. Here we come to the notion of the integration of subjects in a topic.

Integration of subject matter

We have pointed out that one of the aims of early years education is to introduce children to socially valued knowledge, which, it has been suggested, takes as its starting point the subject matter found in the National Curriculum. It is argued in the working party reports that each subject in the National Curriculum has its own knowledge claims, principles and ways of thinking. Young children can be introduced to these in ways which are suitable to their level of development and ways of thinking. It is also evident that one subject frequently has a close relationship to another. For instance, the proposals of the Secretary of State for Education and Science in *History for Ages 5–16* (DES 1990b) has a chapter on the relationships between history and the remainder of the curriculum. This chapter also contains a warning:

> The cross curricular process is two way: the subject of history can benefit from the insights, knowledge and methods of other subjects just as it can and should contribute to them. This cross fertilisation must not however be allowed to lead to any loss of rigour and the distinctive nature and methods of history must not be compromised.
>
> (DES 1990b)

Integration of subject matter in a manner which does not do justice to individual subjects can take place and has come under criticism. Other criticisms of integrated topic work include the suggestion that it can be confusing to children. It is necessary, therefore, to take a careful look at integration to identify when and how it can be justified.

It has been argued that young children look on the world and therefore learn about it in a holistic way because 'the environment is manifestly an integrated one and as such it should be treated' (Oliver 1975). We have already agreed that there are connections which can be made between subjects. However, we have also suggested that each subject has distinctive ways of thinking. Taken together, these make the notion of artificial barriers irrelevant. However, if a holistic view is taken to its extreme, it can be suggested that, in school, young children may be constrained in their learning by being introduced to subjects. That is, learning any subject, such as science, separately, divorces this subject from its natural connections with other areas of experience and distorts the way children think. This view can lead to statements such as 'It is important that the natural flow of activity, imagination, language and thought be uninterrupted by artificial breaks such as subject matter' (infant school memorandum quoted in Alexander 1984). This memorandum is, of course, very problematic. Children can hardly think or talk in a context-free vacuum. More seriously, we need to consider, first whether it can be proved to be the case that children think holistically and, second what a 'natural connection' between subjects might involve.

It is not entirely clear what a 'holistic' view of the world might mean nor whether children employ it. Children and adults do develop individual pictures of the world in their minds formed by their cultures, their education and all their various experiences. In effect we can do no other. Those parts of the picture we draw on to communicate, or to make decisions, or to learn are no doubt affected by the whole but are not necessarily 'holistic'. Even if children do have such a view, which seems doubtful, or if it could be defined, which seems unlikely, it does not seem to be a justification for organising knowledge as if everything could be presented at once. The environment may 'manifestly' be integrated but no one can attend to all its manifestations at the same time.

If integration is taken to extremes based on a 'holistic' view of how children learn, teachers might attempt to bring every area of experience together in one topic. This may lead to planning which fragments knowledge and learning into a superficial treatment of all the content, so that confusion rather than integration may reign.

With regard to our second question, concerning the 'natural' connection between the subjects in the curriculum, it seems that natural connections can be identified which are extremely tenuous. That is, almost anything can be shown to have a natural connection with almost anything else that could be taught. To illustrate what we mean let us take the handy but treacherous system of brainstorming the content of a topic. If anything that comes to mind is included we can fall into the trap of word association. It is a trap because words that are connected in one person's mind are not necessarily connected in the mind of anyone else and the connection may be bizarre. Recently, we saw a topic book which included, amongst other things on a theme of water, evaporation and Jesus walking on the water. The absurdity of this connection can be seen more clearly if 'salt' is substituted for 'water'. There is still a 'natural' connection. Salt is left if salty water is evaporated and Jesus undoubtedly walked on water that was salty. It is possible to have integration which flies in the face of common sense. No sensible connection is being made between subject areas or anything else. Moreover, in this example children would be likely to have separate sessions or lessons in science and religious education so any purpose for including these two in one topic would be hard to identify. There are natural connections to be made in topics between areas of experience or subjects but these should be more than what springs into the mind on first thought.

Furthermore, integrated work can be criticised because it does not take the knowledge claims of subjects seriously (Alexander *et al.* 1992) Her Majesty's inspectors have been particularly critical of confusing connections being made between history and geography (DES 1978). A culprit here is the shortage of good material for teachers, including information books. It is not difficult to find packs for teachers on, for example, 'homes' which can present children with an incoherent mixture of castles, igloos, wigwams, tepees, animal habitats and children's own houses. If not selectively used, a mishmash of this sort can hardly be serious about history, geography, science or environmental studies. At the same time each section would lack the necessary depth of study and could present children with unfortunate stereotypes and misinformation which would need to be unlearned later. It is not hard to find similar examples related to 'transport' or 'people who help us', even in books intended for student teachers. We suggest that making tenuous connections between discrete bits of knowledge cannot be justified as integration. It may be useful to look at why this can happen.

The antecendents of 'tenuous' connections in integration

We have suggested various reasons why inappropriate integrated work appears in schools. These included the assumption that children think in holistic ways and that artificial barriers will impede their learning, or the fear that infant teaching could become traditional as opposed to progressive. Traditional teaching could be thought of as subject centred, formal, instructional, and with children seated in rows. Progressive teaching could be thought to be child centred, informal, oriented to discovery learning and to use group and individual teaching. We would question whether at any level of education it is sensible to divide approaches to teaching in this way. All teachers teach content and all teachers teach children. 'I teach children not subjects' is a slogan which bears little examination. Teachers of young children may be worried that their curriculum becomes a watered-down version of secondary teaching. This fear cannot be met by being reluctant to teach children anything which might be labelled as knowledge. An attempt to be child centred (and it does no justice to secondary colleagues to suggest that they are not child centred) does not justify presenting children with confusion. Similarly, teachers may be afraid that the processes of learning may be lost if there is an end product, or if there is any emphasis on knowledge. The processes of learning – learning how to learn – are undoubtedly crucial. There seems to be no reason why these should be lost because there is also a content. Moreover, learning how to learn includes learning in the particular ways that the subjects introduce. Young children, for example, are very capable of weighing up evidence which is, although not exclusively so, the province of both history and science.

Although we respect those teachers who feel able to meet the demands of the National Curriculum and retain a thoroughgoing process approach to the curriculum focusing on skills, we are not sure that this can work in the real world of the classroom. One commentator points out

> Instead of an elementary stock of knowledge and skills this teacher [working in a process framework] has to know how to stimulate and organise the thinking and doing of a whole class in such a way as to lead to the collective formulation of a problem, one that has the potential for other and more stimulating problems in its turn, one that 'matches' effectively the powers of the group as a whole, yet allows individuals to play suitable parts. Then having made that selection, he or she has to know how to provide for or at least suggest means for the solution of the problem and satisfactory ways in which the parts played by the individuals concerned can be worked out so their own knowledge is thereby extended.
>
> (Blyth 1984)

We have rarely seen anything remotely like this in action but our point is that some attempts to retain these ideals may have degenerated into justifications for integrated work of the sort we have been criticising. While making it clear that the processes of learning are important, we maintain that the content of learning is equally important and that it is possible to deal with both aspects in sensibly integrated topic work.

The practical and realistic integration of content into topics

We have described topic work which, we have argued, can be confused and confusing. We suggest that to avoid these pitfalls the content of a topic should consist of areas of the curriculum which are linked by more sensible criteria than what we have called 'word association'. It is evident that Her Majesty's inspectors have been most impressed by topics which are not over-diffuse.

> While most schools teach history and geography through topic work much of the best practice occurs when such an approach involves a detailed study which is predominantly historical or geographical in nature rather than integrating several subjects around some general theme.
>
> (DES 1989a)

and

> Many Primary schools approach the teaching of science through topic work which involves aspects of other subjects such as history or geography. In the best circumstances this approach provides scope for developing children's knowledge skills and understanding in science. However where such topic work is not well planned, or when too

many aspects of different subjects are attempted, the work often lacks coherence and as a result the children receive a superficial experience of science.

(DES 1989b)

Of course, even if a topic is predominantly centred around a single subject, cross curricular skills and knowledge will be involved. We teach in English and through English. Children will read, write, talk and listen about the theme. Those whose mother tongue is not English will also do so, using what they have already learned about language – which is considerable – as they gain experience of English. Similarly young children will paint, draw, act, calculate, measure, observe, communicate, solve problems and so on. If a topic is designed to focus on one particular subject, however, the guiding principle should be that the experiences children are given should illuminate or add a dimension to that subject. A similar principle would apply to each subject if more than one is selected as a unifying theme.

Clearly more than one subject can profitably be included in a topic. Subjects do interrelate and there are sensible relationships between mathematics and science, drama and history, science and technology, geography, environmental studies and economic and industrial understanding. The list could go on and on, but not indefinitely and not to the point of tenuous connections. The criteria to consider are whether each subject included adds a dimension to the understanding of the other subjects, and whether the principles of each subject are preserved. A topic for young children on say, the 25th anniversary of the school might have a historical focus. However, it would also include language and probably some geography. Physical education might explore how this subject has changed in 25 years. The subjects included arise naturally in this example. They are part of the topic because they are necessary to its content.

It is important, however, to keep in mind the knowledge claims of those subjects which are often used in support of topics; English is one of course, as are art, PE, music, technology and so on. Let us consider one of these: art. It could be very easy to use art for illustrations and to forget the development and progression of art itself. In a broad and balanced curriculum, a place can probably be made for most subjects or groups of related subjects to be the major focus of a topic at least once. Alternatively, extra work outside of topics might be needed.

Nothing we have said so far prevents teachers from using unifying themes which are not, at first glance, subject centred. Indeed it is important to make links between children's experience and interests and the content of topics. The theme of a topic may be 'toys' or 'change' or 'the teddy bears' picnic'. Many such themes spring to mind. Often they are time honoured because they appeal to young children and relate to but are not limited to what they already know. However, each theme might be examined to ensure that they stand the sort of scrutiny we have been describing. A wealth of exciting experiences for young children in topics can still avoid those pitfalls. Even then it might not be possible to do justice to the whole curriculum. This brings us to the issue of curriculum coverage.

Topic work and the coverage of the curriculum

It has become clear that a topic will not cover all areas of the curriculum at once. There is a curriculum to be covered but the suggested allocations of time made by the various National Curriculum working parties are equivalents. That is, whereas a secondary school might decide to allocate the suggested 3–4 periods a week to history, the early years school will have to decide on an equivalent but not on a daily, weekly or monthly basis. The whole of the early years curriculum will have to be planned with suitable allocations of time in mind. It would be foolish to throw away one of the traditional advantages of teaching young children – that they can spend extended periods on the one theme. In the early years classroom children do not have to stop doing an interesting piece of writing or an experiment at the sound of a bell. This flexibility enables exploration at some depth and, within reason, extension of planned time to include children's interests and meet their strengths. Nevertheless, it is possible to spend too long on a topic. This can occur where a primary school has a common theme, perhaps for a whole term, which may become tedious for young children. It is probably more profitable to consider what is to be covered and then decide on the likely time needed and to vary this perhaps from as little as three weeks to up to half a term. Teachers will be anxious to introduce the children to the whole of the curriculum specified. The sensible integration of topics may be a very good way to include a good deal of the subject matter.

A practical argument for using topics is that it might otherwise be difficult to meet the coverage demanded by the National Curriculum. Nevertheless we suggest that it is neither possible nor desirable to attempt to deal with the whole of the curriculum in topics. In practice this has very rarely been done, for very good reasons. One of them is our own principle that areas of the curriculum should not be dragged into a topic without sensible or necessary connection. Other reasons relate to the need for many activities to be ongoing and continuous. Amongst others, one such activity is learning to read. The range of fiction available would be very limited if always tied into a topic. Other examples can be found. Although many of the children's interests and contributions would be catered for in a topic, some of these might need to be responded to in an immediate way. Certain curriculum areas might be judged to need regular practice and enrichment. Certain concepts, for example time, days of the week, and seasons might need daily reinforcement. If aspects of development in a subject are not fully catered for in topics they will need specific attention. We have mentioned art. If that or any other foundation subject can not be developed properly in topics, further work needs to be implemented separately.

Children's choice and their exploration and mastery of materials engendered by the normal classroom equipment often arise in a topic. But if equipment such as sand, water, constructional toys and the like are not to be used in a topic there is every reason why they should continue to be enjoyed outside of it. We see topic work as a major element in the early years curriculum but never as a limitation of it. Children's learning is too important to be tied to a single style of teaching.

Children's learning and topic work

So far we have examined topic work mainly but not exclusively in terms of content and as a way of teaching. It has not been possible to separate these aspects from children's learning, nor would we have wished to do this. Now we wish to concentrate on what we know or begin to know about how young children learn, in order to consider whether using topics in the curriculum has any special advantages in meeting children's cognitive strengths and needs. We shall begin with a brief overview of some of the evidence we have about how children learn.

This is not a book on the psychology of learning. Nevertheless, any attempt to discuss classroom practice has to take into account current learning theories and research evidence. That which seems most convincing describes learning as a complex process which is, in effect, rather messy. That is, it is neither straightforward nor linear (Bennett *et al.* 1984, Desforges 1989, Nicholls *et al.*, 1989) Children do not seem to learn in a step-by-step manner. Common sense indicates that some learning is dependent on previous acquisition; you cannot, for example, add within ten before you can count within ten. However, concepts seem to be built up in a piecemeal fashion. New information is gathered, old theories are rejected or refined and conflicts are sorted out as children construct various conceptual schemata. No single learning theory appears to give a convincing explanation of this process, which is still fairly mysterious.

[T]here is a huge literature on the nature of learning under different conditions. This provides illustrations of imitation, social modelling, rote, invention, construction, discovery and practice. Of course this literature is already presented to student teachers. Unfortunately it frequently appears in debates about the nature of learning (discovery versus reception for example). However, we are beginning to learn that learning is multi-faceted; that learning can and does take all these forms and each form has a role to play in the development of the intellect and the acquisition of knowledge.

(Desforges 1989)

What is known with some certainty is the sorts of things children have shown themselves to be capable of before they come to school. There is a considerable literature deriving from research which indicates that developmental psychologists 'now regard the young child as being intellectually much more competent than was previously thought' (Hughes 1989). The work of developmental psychologists and that of other educationists has for the most part focused on preschool children. Work on emergent literacy (children's attainments in language before school) is proceeding in both the United Kingdom and the United States. Tizard and Hughes (1984) have investigated the conversations which take place at home between pre-school girls and their mothers. In general, these were more productive and far ranging than conversations in nursery school. The authors were particularly impressed by passages of 'intellectual search' in homes, where the young children pursued conversational topics in some depth, aided by an interested adult.

Among many studies of the acquisition of spoken language Gordon Wells's work in Bristol led him to conclude that:

all but a small minority of children reach the age of schooling with a vocabulary of several thousand words, control of the basic grammar of their community and an ability to deploy these resources in conversations arising from the many and varied situations that occur in their everyday lives.

(Wells 1978)

It is not only in spoken language that children learn before school. Nicholls *et al.* (1989), in an action research project conducted by classroom teachers, replicated the view of Ferreiro and Teberosky (1982) that many children come to school knowing a good deal about the process of writing.

In the area of mathematics, Hughes (1986) found that young children understand small numbers and number operations presented to them as games. Work in our own university (Aubrey and Pettitt in progress) with new entrants to reception classes has found that young children frequently have a powerful grasp of many of the mathematical concepts embodied in level 1 of Key Stage 1 of the National Curriculum in mathematics. These include the ability to count and represent numbers in a variety of ways, to use spatial language accurately and to give sensible explanations related to early concepts of probability. We can also mention, for example, the work of Gelman and Gallistel (1978) which indicates that preschoolers can conserve small numbers and that of Desforges and Desforges (1980) which showed that young children of 3 and 4 can deal with the division of numbers up to 20 and are inventive in coping with remainders.

These examples, selected from many studies, indicate that young children are remarkably good at learning. Obviously, although all children are good at learning, some are much better than others and some have had better opportunities for learning before school. Individual differences are not necessarily related to social class. Most of the studies referred to above crossed over class boundaries. Although it is the case that, overall, working class children do not do as well as middle-class children in school, the former can succeed and the can latter fail. Nor is it the case that children from one-parent families or broken homes will fail in school. Teachers may be helped in their work if they are aware of circumstances which may affect a child's learning. Their job, however, is not to see home background as determining success or failure but to take children as they are and to enable them to learn. The varying nature of what children can do when they come to school does not affect our argument that all have the ability to learn given the opportunity.

It may be helpful to consider how children learn in their homes, given a parent who can, and does take time to listen and answer questions. We referred earlier to the passages of 'intellectual search' identified by Tizard and Hughes (1984). One such passage took the form of several conversations where a child was struggling to understand ideas about work, payment and earning. At the beginning she believed that a window cleaner paid his clients and not the other way round. The final recorded conversation took this form:

Mother: I expect the window-cleaner's going to have his lunch now.
Child: He would have all that much lunch (stretches arms out wide) because he's been working all the time.
Mother: Mm . . . I expect he gets very hungry doesn't he? I expect he goes to the pub and has some beer and sandwiches.
Child: He has to pay for that.
Mother: Yes, he does.
Child: Not always though.
Mother: Mm . . . always.
Child: Why not?
Mother: They won't give him any beer and sandwiches if he doesn't have any money.
Child: But why doesn't he use his own food?

(Tizard and Hughes 1984)

Tizard and Hughes comment that the child's concepts about work and payment are still unclear. The child has the 'intellectual capacity' and her mother's explanations are uncomplicated. However, they suggest that: 'this conversation reveals something which is characteristic of the slow and gradual way in which a child's understanding of an abstract or complex topic is built up' (ibid.).

This extract demonstrates a child's persistent attempt to make sense of her world and the gradual development of concepts. She exemplifies our point that children, given the opportunity, are good learners. Simply because they are good at learning, their concepts have to be built up gradually over time. In order to understand the complexities before them, they need the opportunity to ask the endless questions that come into their minds, and space and time to think. Questions arise when the context – what is happening – is meaningful to the child. This brings us back to the subject of topic work. It seems likely that a topic, with its in-depth exploration of a theme, can provide opportunities for teaching and learning which are similar to those which have been found at home. Teachers, however, have a problem not found in homes: that of dealing with thirty or so children at once. They cannot often take advantage of unstructured or unintended happenings. They can, however, set up a well-planned topic which provides a purposeful context in which children are given time to learn and which gives them an incentive to question. A topic is a way of working which, to repeat an earlier premise, makes sense to the participants. It also provides the necessity to perform certain actions. That is, the topic provides reasons for what is being done.

In research into the mathematics children bring to school (Aubrey and Pettitt in progress) it was found that although many children attain basic mathematical concepts by the time they reach school age others do not. For example, although many children could count and understand the principles of counting (one to one correspondence, cardinality, order irrelevance) some children could not count at all. The former, however, had presumably not acquired their knowledge by colouring in, or putting rings round objects or drawing lines from eggs to egg cups. These activities are rarely found in nurseries or homes. What we are suggesting is that children who could count had learned to do so where they felt it necessary and reasonable to count and were helped to do so. Those children who could not count might not need to learn differently, although they might well not be so good at learning as their more able peers and, very likely, have had less support at home. One way to teach them might be to provide a topic where it made sense to count.

Earlier we discussed the multi-faceted nature of learning. Although topic work may not be the only way to provide multi-faceted learning experiences, it seems reasonable to suggest that it can be a very good way to do so. It is certainly possible to provide a content in topics which is highly motivating for young children.

SUMMARY

We have discussed the teacher's task in the infant classroom and given our views about how topic work may be used to meet the problems of implementing the National Curriculum. We have identified those features of a topic which we believe are crucial to honouring content, retaining the processes of learning and matching how children learn. In our chapters devoted to exemplifying topics we shall illustrate how those features may be adhered to in practice.

Chapter 2

Planning, organisation and assessment of the curriculum

INTRODUCTION

In this chapter and subsequent chapters, the key roles of planning and organisation will be discussed. It is hardly possible to separate these issues, both of which include assessment. Planning the content of the curriculum extends into planning how that curriculum shall be implemented and the organisation of the school and the classroom for that purpose. The organisation of the school and the classroom, in turn, affects and constrains content.

The overall framework of the content of the curriculum is given by the National Curriculum. Nevertheless, there is more to planning within that framework than looking at the various attainment targets. It is expected by the Department for Education that the programmes of study for each subject will be used to plan detailed content which will eventually enable children to meet attainment targets. The programmes of study are not schemes of work: these have to be drawn up by teachers. Schools must also make decisions about how the schemes of work they write will be organised and implemented. Within these decisions will be a consideration of whether topics should be used in the curriculum and if so, how this will be done.

There is little doubt that there is concern about how successful the continued use of topics will be in meeting the aims of the National Curriculum. As pointed out in chapter 1, widespread discussion and concern, heavily covered in the media, culminated in the 1991 commission, by the then Secretary of State for Education, of an investigation into primary education by Robin Alexander, Jim Rose and Chris Woodhead (the so-called 'three wise men'). This followed research by one of them into primary education in Leeds (Alexander 1992). A result of the deliberations of the three wise men was the publication of a discussion paper on primary education (Alexander et al. 1992), which subsequently, as was intended, became the subject of fierce debate. This is an indication of the intensive spotlight focused on primary education. The use of topics and, if they are used, what they should be like, is an important issue striking at the heart of accepted practice.

It is probably true that it is difficult to ensure that school schemes of work for each subject can be utilised effectively when they are amalgamated into topics. Schools have to plan their curricula over an extended period and working topics into them is not easy. However, the fact that something is accepted to be difficult is not a reason or an excuse for abandoning it, if experience can indicate that it is worth doing. Nevertheless, it is important to acknowledge the difficulties and look carefully at the problems. This chapter attempts to do so and is written with the benefit of liaison with schools which have encountered and made headway in dealing with the problems.

It has been and will be made explicit that our experience indicates that topics cannot cover the whole of the curriculum without distortion of content. It is also likely that broad-based topics are those in which it is most difficult to arrange curriculum coverage and that subject-focused topics will be needed for at least some sections of the curriculum. School planning of overall coverage needs to consider this view. As noted above and in chapter 1, topics can be unsatisfactory for a number of reasons and it is not intended to repeat these reservations. However, they will affect suggestions made in this chapter about planning and organisation. Obviously, any school will have particular views and circumstances which will affect their deliberations and decisions. We shall be painting a broad picture, highlighting those issues which seem important. Further issues about planning and organisation will arise in the chapters which follow and will be dealt with there.

This chapter will add to the plethora of advice, exhortation, suggestion and criticism addressed to teachers about planning and organisation in classrooms, where after all they – the teachers – are the experts. Teachers' jobs extend, more than is often accepted or realised outside the profession, into the pre-active and post-active realm. In other words they work very long hours. All of the advice and all this work mean nothing unless the whole point of the exercise is kept in mind. This point is that at which a teacher teaches (in the full sense of this all-embracing word) and a child or children learn in the classroom. We shall try to keep this principle in mind.

ELEMENTS OF CURRICULUM PLANNING AND CLASSROOM ORGANISATION

A search of the literature on curriculum planning and its partner, organisation, reveals that certain elements can be identified which planners need to consider (see Morrison and Ridley 1988 for a review). Drawing on this literature we can identify key elements in curriculum planning.

Examples will be given and some general comments will be made. This outline will provide some definitions and background for further observations. These observations will focus mainly on content and assessment of the curriculum in the section on school planning but will all be used in the sections on classroom planning and organisation.

In planning a curriculum, the content – what is to be taught – is an overriding element. There is a difference of emphasis to be noted within content. What children are to do is not synonymous with what it is hoped that they will learn from that activity. Schools have to plan what they intend children to learn with reference to the programmes of study. These plans become schemes of work for each subject, containing experiences and activities which provide specific purposes for learning. Translating the knowledge, skills and understandings to be learned from these schemes into activities that children will do is a classroom task and it is here that a problem may arise. Children may be asked to read a book or write a story, for example, but the teacher's intentions about what the children are to learn from either of these activities may take many different forms. Of course, what children actually learn may not match the teacher's intentions; however, that does not alter the teacher's responsibility to identify purposes for learning.

Assessment of learning is not separate from, but has to be built into, the planning of content. Planning has to be made with assessment in mind, including, some would say unfortunately, standardised national testing at the age of 7. The attainment targets of the National Curriculum vary rather widely. In some cases they can be broken down into their component parts, and each part can be identified as an objective. In other cases, the attainment targets look like processes, where a concept is built up slowly over time. Examples of the former sort can be found in attainment target 2 level 1 (*Mathematics in the National Curriculum*, DES 1991a) and of the latter in attainment target 3 level 2 (*History in the National Curriculum*, DES 1991c). In turn, assessment is likely to look rather different depending on the type of learning outcome which is predicted. Deciding what forms assessment should take is part of planning. A further element of curriculum planning to be considered is the availability of resources.

Resources can be classified under the headings of personnel, time, space and materials. Each category impinges on the others but will be looked at separately as each is important in its own right. Resources are often a constraint on planning. The deployment of resources of all kinds is often a matter for decisions by headteachers, usually in consultation with staff, but the buck (and local management of schools) stops at their desks. The management responsibilities of headteachers are also factors which are not always taken into account, outside of the profession, when comments are made about class size or the failure of schools to meet expectations.

The personnel or people resource in a school centres on the teaching staff. Planning for the deployment of this crucial and expensive resource involves difficult decisions about class size, year or mixed age groups and curriculum responsibilities, to name but a few of these problems. Others relate to how to share scarce ancillary help, school policies about parental involvement and the help obtainable from and given to students in initial teacher education, secondary school placements and others learning about schools such as NNEB (Nursery Nurses Examination Board) students. After global decisions have been made, year groups and class teachers have to plan how to make use of any help they have been allocated.

The availability of time is the resource which teachers usually claim most constrains what they can do. Such a scarce and limited commodity demands a good deal of thought. Exercises carried out in schools on the use of time have often been revealing; it is found that a troubling proportion of time is spent on activities which can only remotely be described as cognitive. These findings are in agreement with research data by Tizard *et al.* (1988). Inevitably considerable time has to be spent, for example, in moving children around the school. Nevertheless, a staff development day spent on rethinking items such as the position of the fixed points in the day (assemblies, television, playtimes and dinner hours) may be productive.

This brings us to the resource of space. In some schools space is at a premium, others have a good deal at their disposal. In either event priorities for the use of space have to be identified. Flexibility may be a key consideration. The use of space is strongly connected to the use of materials. Some schools have evolved a practice of moving children from one room to another, on a weekly basis, to make best use of all their resources. This is obviously a radical notion, causing a good deal of upheaval, but it is an experiment demonstrating flexible thinking.

Less controversially, schools with extra space may be able to double up use of spare classrooms as they consider whether the pressing need is for parents' rooms, a music room, a resources room, a design and technology area or perhaps all of these. Where space is tight, dual or triple use of what is available may be considered. Space in schools is so variable that it can only be touched on by suggesting that it requires constant review. This, of course, is often forced on schools by falling or rising rolls.

Materials include consumables (paper, paint, etc.), equipment, books, commercially produced schemes and furniture of all kinds. Constraining all of these is the financial management of the school, which also has to include the major items of salaries and maintenance, all of which add to headteachers' headaches. What is available already and what priorities there are for new materials is integral to planning the curriculum and so is the money which would be needed for visits and visitors. The financial help schools must seek from parents directly or indirectly through sales and the like is invaluable and this is not the place to discuss whether schools should have to seek this help. It may not be appropriate either, to debate whether or not the maintained sector would fall apart if all teachers removed their personal property from classrooms. What is clear is that resources can limit the curriculum.

All the elements of curriculum planning which have been mentioned have to be evaluated regularly. Such evaluations may be ongoing but they should also be built into cycles of curriculum planning and range from the day-to-day evaluations of classroom practice to overall evaluations of school schemes of work. None can be omitted and all hinge on the effectiveness they have had on learning.

Most of the points made in this section state the obvious. However, it is stressed that planning and organisation are dynamic processes. Everyone in the teaching business, at every level knows they can never think that the problems have been solved. It cannot all be taken back to the drawing board and none of us can afford to take a plan out of a drawer, blow off the dust, and do it again. The consolation may be that teaching and planning for teaching is never boring.

WHOLE SCHOOL PLANNING OF CONTENT

In addressing the planning of whole school content, we make the assumption that schools intend to include topics in the curriculum. Before topics can evolve, however, the knowledge, skills and understandings for each subject at each level need to be identified. It is being suggested that, where National Curriculum documents have been published, they should be starting points for planning. (Otherwise, in religious education, for example, guidance such as Agreed Syllabuses should be used.) No doubt it is possible to think of topics and identify their potential to embody necessary learning experiences. Nevertheless, starting from topics is very likely to make for both gaps and overlap in the curriculum. As time goes on, teachers will know that certain topics are adequate. However, it might be argued that there is more scope for diversity and variation in topics if fresh ideas can be generated from the necessary coverage. Favourite topics need not be abandoned but teachers might consider not what learning can arise from a topic on, say, food, but where in the schemes of work would such a topic map onto what it is intended to teach.

In order to make these decisions, school schemes of work are required for each subject. As noted above, schemes of work are drawn from the programmes of study and should lead to the meeting of attainment targets. A way of planning which many schools are adopting is to devolve responsibility for each subject to members of staff. Where there are curriculum coordinators, they would be the persons involved. Of course, in a small school other staff would be drawn in and, realistically, a member of staff may have more than one subject to deal with. Nevertheless, it does not seem sensible to ask individual teachers to work out schemes of work for all subjects.

To avoid repetition, members of staff (which may include the head-teacher) with responsibility for drawing up a scheme of work, will be called curriculum leaders. The schemes of work they develop, in consultation with the headteacher and colleagues, are more than a policy statement. A policy statement is generally concerned with broad aims; schemes of work include those aims but are worked up into detailed objectives derived from pro-grammes of study and the attainment targets. Further revision is necessary as the National Curriculum changes and probably after the implementation of the curriculum for a three-year cohort in the infant phase. Schools using this system do, of course, approve the overall scheme before it is ready for classroom use. Then each curriculum leader consults with class teachers and year groups to decide jointly how the schemes are to be implemented and assessed. Clearly there will be a certain amount of role switching, but most teachers will welcome shared responsibilities which empower them and either develop existing subject expertises or allow new strengths to be acquired. At least one primary school we know has a nursery teacher as its mathematics curriculum leader. As promotion is likely to be based more on subject expertise in the future, teachers may well welcome this sort of opportunity.

In this system further responsibility and autonomy is given to teachers so that, subject to the framework and checks which have been described, they can use their own individual experiences and expertise as a generalist to best effect. Given this freedom of style and method (within sensible limits) teachers may be at their best in enabling children to learn. They will be able to decide, with the agreement of the curriculum leader, what topics they intend to use and what other work will be needed to cover the curriculum for each class. All of the work planned will almost certainly have to relate to more than one National Curriculum level. However, the topics teachers select will be different from those selected for other year groups. New topics can cover the same concepts as ones taught before but with content which appears to be different in the eyes of children so that they will not think 'I've done that'. Naturally, devolving decisions about choice of topics to teachers requires that detailed and specific records are kept of each topic for the information of the whole school.

This system is, of course, only one of the many which schools have adopted for their overall planning. It seems to work well in practice and its advantages have been outlined. No doubt others work just as well but some have problems which will be examined. As far as topics are con-cerned, some schools, worried about how to get science into the curri-culum, have decreed that all their thematic work shall be science based. This is problematic for a number of reasons. The first is related to the arguments which have been made about subjects in the curriculum. It has been suggested that subjects have distinctive knowledge bases, principles and ways of thinking. To have a curriculum based on any one subject, therefore, may distort both that subject and those pulled in to support it. Electricity and magnetism seem to be a common choice of content in this way of organising the curriculum and of course this is a valid topic. However, it is hard to see how all the subjects in the curriculum could or should be included in it. In a study of electricity, one might include history of kitchen equipment. However, unless this were a properly developed, new theme or sub-theme, once-over-lightly, one-off sessions might be inevitable. This criticism might be extended to making any subject drive the curriculum. In a recent schools broadcast it was suggested that the whole curriculum could be derived from design and technology. No doubt the whole curriculum could be derived from anything one cares to dream up, but the cost in terms of confused children might be high.

There are further disadvantages to prescription of whole school topics. For example, if all classes are told what topics are to be used for each half term, the implications for use of materials are serious. More importantly, the curriculum cycle comes under strain. To take electricity and magnetism as an example again, if this were a whole school project it might not be repeated again during a three-year cycle. In that event what knowledge would reception class children have of the topic at age 7? Moreover, there are questions about appropriateness and length of a topic. *History in the National Curriculum* (DES 1991c) is a two-year programme at Key Stage 1. In this subject and perhaps for others, reception teachers are working with an eye to level 1 but not altogether within level 1. It might be much better for reception classes to have mostly broad-based topics, where in the example of history, the language of time is being inculcated through stories, than to have full-blown subject-focused topics. In reception classes, attention might be focused more productively on basic skills, albeit learned in topics appealing to very young children. This is a matter for individual school decisions but it should also be borne in mind that the length of any topic might need to be varied according to the age of the children and the possibilities of holding their interest. Topics lasting for half a term may simply be too long for young children. Of course, one thing may lead to another but there is a curriculum to be covered which must be planned. Going where a topic leads because it has been prescribed for too long a period may not be a good use of time. Again, devolving selection and length of a topic to the judgement of a class teacher may be productive. She or he is in the best position to judge where saturation point has been reached and when children are not learning any more from a topic.

Nothing written above prevents a school from embarking on a whole school project for a limited period (which might be a different period for some age groups). A topic on the local environment or responding to a local event can be very exciting. (Schools in the north-east in 1992 were festooned with red and white banners and names of footballers when Sunderland were in the FA cup. Unfortunately they lost!) More seriously – but not for Sunderland FC – there are some good descriptions of whole school topics in *Aspects of Primary Education: the Teaching and Learning of History and Geography* (DES 1989a).

At school planning level, overall decisions have to be taken about assessment. Curriculum leaders may be responsible for drawing up schedules of key attainment to be assessed in their subjects. Some of these can be drawn almost directly from attainment targets but there is enormous variability between subjects. In mathematics, for example, in attainment target 2 level 1 (DES 1991a), a huge number of objectives can be identified from the programmes of study and the attainment target is ludicrously limited. It is beyond our scope to examine all these differences, although some reference will be made to them in the subject chapters. Nevertheless, schools have to examine each attainment target and identify whether it is specific, whether it can be broken down into more specific items, or whether it looks much more like an ongoing process. We suspect that there must be a continuous review as schools evolve their assessment procedures and we have to say that some of the non-statutory examples of attainment given in the various documents are misleading and inappropriate. School discussions of better examples might be very useful. Schools, however, must produce schedules for the aggregation of the more informal records a class teacher makes with more formal teacher assessment for every school year. Teacher assessments at age 7 are a legal requirement, although they are disregarded where a standard attainment target differs from them (with certain exceptions requiring many conditions to be met). The job of class 2 teachers is impossible unless teacher assessments in each preceding year are rigorous. Therefore, common agreed records are essential. The suggestions made in documents issued to schools by the School Examination and Assessment Council to this end are useful. Schools also have to decide on the content of files to be kept for each child and the nature of the evidence which is to be included. More will be said about teachers' day-to-day assessment in the next section.

CLASSROOM PLANNING

Overall school planning, whatever form it takes and however good it is, stands or falls on the ability of the classroom teachers to elaborate the planning for their classes and to manage the children and the learning in the classroom. It has already been suggested that teachers should not be expected to plan directly from the programmes of study. Whether they do this or not, they are at the sharp end of curriculum planning – where it meets children. Suggestions follow about how class teachers might plan.

If a school is large, it may have parallel classes or there may be team teaching (one large class taught by two or more teachers). In this chapter, the term 'class teacher' will be used as a blanket term to cover either an individual teacher or a team of some kind who are planning the same curriculum. Class teachers have to draw up plans and normally an outline is identified for the whole year. This is broken down into school year terms and begins to ensure that the necessary curriculum is covered during the year and that it is balanced. Achieving balance might necessitate decisions about different sorts of topics, but it also requires decisions about the inclusion of subjects – whether in topics or outside of topics, or both – particularly the allocation of time for each, and the themes, issues and dimensions described in *Curriculum Guidance 3 – The Whole Curriculum* (NCC 1990).

Detailed planning should follow for the first term, a process which will have to be repeated in the second and third terms. Planning notes have to be made well in advance in order that resources can be checked, visits organised and materials obtained or booked, for example from Local Education Authority (LEA) sources. At each level of planning more details are incorporated from schemes of work for each subject. The earlier such detail is included the less work has to be done later, but experience indicates that planning has to be revised when it hits the classroom. On the one hand, class teachers have to be flexible, but on the other hand, they must keep curriculum coverage in mind. In spite of the need to cover the curriculum, teachers must also bear in mind that it is important not to rush children. It will stand children in good stead if what is learned is learned well and they are not pushed too rapidly from level to level.

It is likely that headteachers will want to see curriculum plans, probably half termly but possibly more often. It has been suggested in respect of topics that these can be overlong, so a half term plan might include two topics and teachers' additional plan for supplementary content. It is useful at this point to list each of the subjects in the curriculum and to show what is intended to be taught for each, including both topic and supplementary work. For any one half term history and geography might not appear because they will be taught in blocks elsewhere in the year, but the other core and foundation subjects are mandatory.

A half termly plan should also include provision for specific assessment. That is, teachers should show where and how it is intended to assess particular skills, knowledge and understanding following a block of work. A teacher might, for example, wish to assess the language of measurement at level 1, the understanding of the need for standard measures at level 2 or estimation of standard measures informed by experience at level 3 in mathematics. These built-in assessments are in addition to continuous assessment, which will be discussed within our review of organisation. Assessment of a block of work is obviously not possible if no such block exists. This point is made to indicate that assessment becomes very difficult if a topic is too diffuse. For example, if a topic on food has one or two sessions or lessons on where some food comes from, these are unlikely to provide evidence of attainment in geography. This is one reason why we suggest the inclusion of some subject-focused topics which can provide such evidence.

Planning a topic will need to include these built-in assessment points. How a topic is planned can take many forms, some of which are suggested in subsequent chapters, and it is not intended to repeat the caveats of chapter 1. There is no doubt that the topic web is the most common format but it has to be stressed that initial planning of any sort for a topic is initial. That is, it will need to be revised and reformulated in the light of working backwards and forwards to and from schemes of work and the resources of time, place, personnel and materials referred to above. The most important consideration is whether the content includes the intended learning. When topic webs are used, it is useful to augment the original web (which probably sets out what the children will do) with two or more webs. One of these can be what the children will do, mapped onto another which sets out what the children are intended to learn in each subject, and possibly a third related to the themes, issues and dimensions of the whole curriculum (such as personal and social education or multicultural education).

After the topic(s) and supplementary learning have been planned, the starting points, progression, development and assessment have to be decided. Teachers will probaly find it useful to write brief, weekly forecasts related to these plans, but not too far in advance, to allow for flexibility. In training, students are also required to write daily lesson or session plans and plans for the learning purposes embodied in those activities which children may select. Experienced teachers may not need these details although many have informed us that they continue this practice (albeit rather untidily and strictly for their own use). At the least it seems essential to have notes about teaching sessions and provision which make purposes for learning clear. A typical format – but by no means the only one – for a lesson or session would normally have all or some of the following features:

- Content
- Purposes or objectives for the children's learning
- Purposes for the teacher, e.g. assessment or evaluation of a new strategy introduction and development

What the teacher will say, do, explain, exemplify, demonstrate. Questions to be asked

What the children are expected to do: listen, respond, contribute
- Task, action, activity
- Consolidation, e.g. report back, sharing work, marking, discussion
- Follow up
- During and after lesson – assessment and diagnosis

In *The Quality of Pupil Learning Experiences*, Bennett *et al.* (1984) suggest that diagnosis followed by good matching and differentiation require clear purposes for learning. They also note that teachers' intentions for learning do not always map onto what they ask children to do, describing many incidents where teachers thought they were introducing some new learning but the task was actually a matter of practice because the children already knew the skill or concept. Mismatches are also described for tasks too difficult for slow learners, or too easy for high attainers. As Alexander *et al.* (1992) point out in their discussion paper: 'The idea that at any one time learning tasks in nine subjects can be exactly matched to the needs and abilities of all the pupils in a class is hopelessly unrealistic'. However, it may be impossible to match at all if in the cycle of lesson/task – assessment/diagnosis – lesson/task teachers lose sight of their intentions for learning. Teachers also have to organise the class well in order that at least some of these intentions will be effective.

CLASSROOM ORGANISATION

Having made some suggestions about classroom planning, attention will now be directed to 'organisational strategies' and 'teaching techniques'. These terms were used by Alexander *et al.* (1992), but this does not imply that we agree with many or all of the conclusions drawn by this discussion paper. It merely means that the issues raised are important and give us a framework.

'Organisational strategies' is the term used to describe structure, that is, whether the children are taught together as a class, or in smaller groups or individually. Clearly, decisions about structuring depend entirely on what 'is appropriate to the task in hand' (Alexander *et al.* 1992). In the early years class there is always a good deal of class teaching – in music, PE, and story time for example – but it may be worth considering whether or not class teaching can be both extended and improved. It is likely that more elements of the curriculum could be taught to a class productively than is presently the case. There are disadvantages to be acknowledged – teaching to the middle range, general mismatch and inattentiveness – but there are some activities which the class might not experience at all without class teaching. Certain demonstrations, for example, those using lighted candles or requiring large amounts of time and equipment, may only be possible with a class. Moreover, children cannot discover everything in the curriculum, and it is economic of their time and teachers' if they can select some of the curriculum for class teaching. This requires skills of exposition, the ability to give relevant examples and an enthusiasm which will hold the children's attention and interest. It is likely that teachers can do this well if they are interested in and know a lot about the area they are teaching.

In the model which was suggested for a lesson plan, consolidation was listed. Consolidation is essential to learning and can be a class activity. For example, it is useless to ask children to measure items in the class, whether length, weight, area, volume or capacity is employed, in order to establish the need for standard units or to show the inexact nature of measurement, unless their activities are consolidated. There must be a session where conclusions are drawn. Similarly, children can share their stories, see if others can interpret their data or show their plans and models in a class session.

On the improvement of existing traditional class sessions, the common practice of extended carpet discussions at the beginning of a day might come under scrutiny. If a session like this at any time of the day lasts – as some do – for 15 minutes to half an hour or more it should not be *ad hoc* in nature. It demands specific learning purposes. Similar attention might be paid to story time.

On teaching in groups Alexander *et al.* (1992) point out that teaching to groups 'above all provides for pupils to interact with each other and their teacher'. This can hardly be disputed. It may not be sensible to have the children sitting in groups and then tell them to be quiet and get on with their work; or at least it should be made clear when seatwork is to be quiet and when conversation is in order. There are some tasks where children are not, strictly speaking, engaged on a common task, but where conversation and consultation are helpful. Writing their own stories, recalled experience or poems is one (Nicholls *et al.* 1989). At other times the children could be working as a group on a common task. That children often sit in groups but rarely work as a group has been pointed out frequently (e.g. Bennett *et al.* 1984, Alexander *et al.* 1992). This is probably because it is not very easy to find common tasks. These might include: working with science equipment, such as circuits or magnets, writing together, discussing plans for visits and visitors, painting or drawing a multi-faceted picture such as a park, dividing up work for a data handling exercise, planning presentations in PE or drama, or making a large model. However, it is not easy either to set up these situations or to get children to cooperate. Children have to be used to working together, first in pairs and then in groups.

It may also be agreed that the discussion paper is correct when it speaks of groups becoming 'counter productive' (Alexander *et al.* 1992) if there are too many activities going on at once. The teacher's role may become 'crisis management' (Bennett et al. 1984) as he or she is besieged from all sides for help, spellings, marking and what to do next. Routines – discussed later – can help, but even then, the larger the class, the more difficult the teacher's juggling act becomes. Teachers attempt to set tasks so that their major input is to one group while other groups are practising or choosing their activities. This is sensible but the more different the activities the more difficult management becomes. In fact, more groups might be better off 'choosing' than wasting time in unnecessary practice or waiting for the teacher. Systems such as job cards can take care of what to do next, but, unless the class is small, they make it very difficult for the teachers to determine when they are going to teach and to whom. There may be something to be said at times for the majority of groups being occupied on the same subject but at different levels. For example, in mathematics one group might be with the teacher tackling new material, another practising yesterday's teaching and another revising with a scheme. At least the teacher can think 'mathematics' rather than having to switch his or her mind from one subject to another. There might also be advantages to all groups doing various art or craft activities together. Where art is one of many activities, all too often there is no teacher participation or intervention. In early years classrooms, self-selection activities and play will be part of the planned curriculum. Teachers are aware that their own roles are crucial in setting up these activities for groups and where possible participating themselves. Play and self-selected activities do provide learning experiences but the role of the adult is vital (Doise and Mugny 1984).

The discussion paper (Alexander et al. 1992) also mentions the constitution of groups – by ability or attainment, friendship or age – and suggests that there are certain tasks which call for teaching to groups of roughly similar attainment. It seems likely, for example, that most mathematical tasks related to number require such groups, whereas some others, such as aspects of shape and space, may not require such explicit matching (and may indeed be activities introduced to a class and then carried out in groups). The danger is, however, that attainment groups can become fixed, sometimes by the assessment of attainment in only one subject, and fixed groups can become streaming and result in self-fulfilling prophesies. It takes a good deal of experience, good management and copious recording to operate groups flexibly, using different constitutions at different times. Nevertheless, this might be an aim. Friendship groups can be productive if levels of attainment do not seem to be a major problem, at least for some tasks. For example, an able child acting as scribe for a group is not held back and has a splendid opportunity to improve personal skills, and in many areas, the less academically oriented child can take the lead for a change.

As the discussion paper indicates, there must be times when teachers can interact with individuals, and they must make time for this to happen. Making time to teach is determined partly by teaching techniques, which the paper defines as: 'the different methods a teacher can use to work with his/her pupils to promote learning' (Alexander *et al.* 1992).

TEACHING SKILLS AND TECHNIQUES

The major criticisms of the discussion paper (Alexander *et al.* 1992) in respect of techniques are that many teachers (a) tend to feel uncomfortable, for ideological reasons, about telling children anything, (b) have low expectations, and (c) do not criticise children's work constructively. It has been made clear that we see a need for exposition by teachers and for work on that skill. It is not necessarily the case, however, that teachers have low expectations of children. If they did it would be detrimental to children's progress and teachers have to beware of making assumptions. Nor is it the case that teachers invariably refuse to criticise children's work constructively. Criticism must not be destructive but children are well aware of the pecking order of attainment in classrooms. The aim might be not to praise what children know is inferior work, but to challenge children to improve on it as far as possible and to support them so that they can.

Leaving these points aside, however, there are several other teaching techniques in the discussion paper worthy of comment. The first is establishment of routines. Routines can become problematic; for example, if teachers habitually practise teaching routines which are not successful and do not re-think their methods or try alternatives. However, those routines related to the management of children as opposed to the management of learning are clearly crucial. Children should have as much responsibility as possible for their own organisation; they should be familiar with routines for clearing up, lining up and what to do if they finish their work. These sorts of routines save teachers' time and sanity but must be consistent. Many teachers take time at the beginning of a school year to establish rules (as few as possible) and routines, and the boundaries set by their norms for acceptable behaviour.

Another teaching skill is connected with the implementation of the curriculum. The discussion paper mentions that much more time in classrooms is spent on the core areas of the curriculum than on any others, but that children spend proportionately less time on task when working on them than they do when working on the rest of the curriculum. This is a point worthy of much thought. Teachers are hardly to be blamed for focusing on core areas in the light of current assessment procedures. However, it may be the case that too much time can be less than profitable and this may be a further justification for using topics. Commenting on indirect teaching, where children work on their own with workbooks and workcards the paper says:

> The balance between indirect and direct teaching needs to be reviewed. We say this because the research evidence demonstrated very clearly that the level of cognitive challenge provided by the teacher is a signifi- cant factor in performance. One way of providing challenge is to set pupils demanding tasks. But equally it is important for teachers to organise their classrooms so that they have the opportunity to interact with their pupils: to offer explanations which develop thinking, to encourage speculation and hypothesis through sensitive questioning, to create above all a climate of interest and purpose.
>
> (Alexander *et al.* 1992)

Topic work itself does not necessarily provide cognitive challenge. How- ever, it does move away from de-contextualised workcards and worksheets and its variation of content may provide opportunities for the ideal state des- cribed at least to be attempted.

It has already been suggested that reasonably good matching and differentiation depend on clear purposes and it is also certain that they depend on good teaching techniques. Teachers have to keep ongoing notes and records of what children can do and have learned. They have to make time to observe and assess so that they can use this information to decide what to do next. To some extent, every act of teaching incorporates an act of assessment. Without this knowledge teachers can hardly move to 'cognitive challenge'. Clearly, 'there is little point in developing an elaborate record keeping system, if the evidence upon which the records are based are inadequate' (Alexander *et al.* 1992) The evidence will include observation, notes of what children say, dated examples or work and such items as paintings and models. However, interacting with a group to further its learning or with an individual child for the same purpose ascertains what the group or children in it know and can then pose a challenge. Or it may be that interacting shows that the child or children do not need a challenge. They do not understand what they are currently doing. In either event the problem is not wholly one of time. Diagnostic teaching is one of the most difficult of classroom skills. One hindrance is that teachers feel they must teach and leap in too early to do so without giving the children time to express what they know and what their problems are. Another is that children, anxious to please, try to guess what the teacher wants them to say rather than thinking about a problem. Furthermore, teachers often feel guilty about taking time for observation and listening to children (Bennett *et al.* 1984). Nevertheless, the package of teaching/assessment/matching is tightly bound together and, although very difficult, may be the most important of teaching techniques to be developed.

We conclude this chapter on planning and organisation with an anecdote illustrating the art of the possible. A visitor to a large reception class one afternoon was struck by the fact that all the children seemed very occupied by activities which appeared to be educational and that he could not see the teacher. She was spotted finally in the book corner listening to a child read. The visitor was confronted by an indignant 4-year-old with a finger on her lips. 'Musn't 'rupt,' she whispered. 'Miss has her readers.'

Chapter 3

History and topic work

A NATIONAL FRAMEWORK

The National Curriculum History Order (DES 1991c), provides Key Stage 1 teachers with a framework within which individual curriculum plans and schemes of work may be devised and implemented. It allows for flexibility, choice of content and methods of teaching and learning whilst aiming to maintain the integrity and intellectual rigour of the subject. This has to be welcomed. Perhaps more than any other curriculum area the teaching of history has been the subject of repeated criticism by Her Majesty's Inspectorate in the context of their views on integrated work and on the proliferation of rather 'vague' projects which are designed to take in every subject on the timetable, often with contrived and tenuous links. It is claimed that few such topics are developed which have history as a discernible and worthwhile core (see, for example, *Aspects of Primary Education: The Teaching and Learning of History and Geography*, DES 1989a). Valid as this criticism might be, few teachers of Key Stage 1 children would doubt that whilst sound historic knowledge, understanding and skills should be developed in an intellectually rigorous way, this does not have to be removed totally from an integrated curriculum structure or topic based approach. Indeed, *History, Non-Statutory Guidance*, (NCC, 1991a) recommends that at Key Stage 1, history may be taught as part of an integrated theme which covers several National Curriculum subjects, as long as the key elements listed in the history programme of study are explicitly identified in the curriculum plan and in any topic.

The purpose of this chapter is to provide and discuss practical suggestions for interpreting the defined core content of history, whilst retaining appropriate elements of integration and cross-curricular development. This is totally in line with Statutory Orders, which take account of cross-curricular development in stating that:

> The programmes of study should enable pupils to develop knowledge and understanding of British, European and World history.

Each study unit should provide opportunities for the development of the knowledge, understanding and skills necessary for each of attainment targets 1, 2 and 3. In each Key Stage, pupils should have opportunities through the programme of study to

- explore links between history and other subjects
- develop information technology capability
- develop knowledge, understanding and skills relating to cross-curricular themes, in particular, citizenship, environmental, health and careers education, and education for economic and industrial understanding.

(DES 1991c)

The programme of study for Key Stage 1 (levels 1–3) requires that: 'Pupils should be given opportunities to develop an awareness of the past and of the ways in which it was different from the present. They should be introduced to historical sources of different types.' The programme of study consists of just one study unit which should be taught throughout the key stage. This unit consists of elements which must be covered to help to develop an awareness of the past and to help learn about the past, for example: stories of various types such as well-known myths and legends, stories about historical events, eye witness accounts of historical events, fictional stories set in the past and the use of historical sources of various types, including artefacts, pictures and photographs, music, adults talking about their own past, written sources, buildings and sites, and computer-based material.

The emphasis is on progressing from familiar situations to those more distant in time and place. Pupils should have opportunities to investigate

- changes in their own lives and those of their family or adults around them
- changes in the way of life of British people since the Second World War
- the way of life of people in a period of the past beyond living memory.

(DES 1991c)

Within the programme of study itself, numerous suggestions are given for further investigation, which could form the basis of cross-curricular topics, e.g. clothes, houses, diet, shops, jobs, transport, entertainment. It is suggested that pupils should be taught about the lives of famous men and women, leading to suggestions for work on rulers, saints, artists, engineers, explorers, inventors, pioneers, and about events of different types, perhaps centenaries, religious festivals, anniversaries, the Gunpowder Plot, the Olympic Games.

Irrespective of how the study unit is taught and whatever topics are chosen, elements need be linked to the three attainment targets and statements of attainment for history, which specify the knowledge, skills and understanding which pupils are expected to have in the key stage. These are (as outlined in Non-Statutory Guidance):

- *AT1 Knowledge and understanding of history*: This has three strands: knowing about and understanding changes in the past; knowing about and understanding the causes and consequences of past events; knowing about and understanding the different features of past societies and how they functioned.
- *AT2 Interpretations of history*: This is concerned with how people interpret or have interpreted past events. It helps pupils realise that history is seen by different people in different ways at different times.
- *AT3 The use of historical sources*: This is concerned with how we know about the past. It develops pupils' ability to acquire evidence about the past from a range of historical sources.

As pointed out in *History, Non-Statutory Guidance*, these provide the teaching and learning objectives for the subject. Only AT1 has 'knowledge' in its title, but this does not mean that knowledge is unimportant in the other attainment targets. In each target it is made clear that pupils will only be able to show attainment if they can demonstrate knowledge of the historical content in the relevant parts of the programme of study. For much of the time teachers will need to teach towards more than one attainment target, either in a topic or in a single task (NCC, 1991a).

Because of the nature of the relationship between attainment targets and programmes of study in history (i.e. attainment targets are the knowledge, skills and understanding which pupils are expected to acquire and programmes of study are the 'matters, skills and processes' required to be taught in order to help pupils reach these targets), it is essential that statements of attainments are used with the programmes of study when tasks are being planned. Again, as the *Non-Statutory Guidance* suggests, statements of attainment indicate the stages through which pupils are likely to progress in order to develop the abilities defined in each attainment target, and teachers should see statements of attainment as targets or objectives related to the overall attainment target of which they are part. This does not mean that they should only develop tasks which are targeted on a particular statement of attainment. Indeed, tasks will often benefit from being related to a number of levels and to more than one attainment target (NCC 1991a).

In line with the general purposes of teaching the subject, history in the first three years of school involves our past and a study of people viewed in a historical dimension. It should lay firm foundations for children's understanding of the passing of time and for helping them to make sense of the world in which they are growing up. As pointed out by Blyth (1989), it is only recently that work has been done in this area showing that certain topics in the past can play a vital part in the intellectual development of young children. Blyth points out that during the formative years from 4 to 7, teachers are concerned to socialise their pupils and help them develop language, number and physical skills.

> They tend to favour an informal, friendly, perhaps unstructured approach, and work beyond the basic number and language tends to be 'one off' experiences and activities enabling the child to take advantage of content and information in the 7–11 years. Therefore, for most infant teachers the past as 'history' has no place.
>
> (Blyth 1989)

She argues that, in line with Donaldson's thinking (1978), the intellectual ability of young children has been underestimated, and that thinking about people and events beyond their immediate selves helps them to 'decentre', forming a much stronger basis for intellectual development. 'Certain parts of the past, both recent and long ago, have a real part to play in some sort of structured way at certain times in the infant curriculum.' (Blyth 1989).

Space does not allow for continuation of a lengthy discussion on the value of or justification for why there is a place for history in the first three years of school. Perhaps the more important question is how is this to be done within the National Curriculum framework as outlined above.

It is helpful to pursue this question in the context of a case study and practical examples of good practice. Indeed, it is perhaps difficult, if not meaningless, to analyse a rationale for the teaching of early years history without specific content to discuss.

HISTORY IN PRACTICE: A CASE STUDY[1]

'Images of our school' is a historical topic planned for Key Stage 1 which aims to develop the concepts of time and change, yet which places considerable emphasis on addressing knowledge, understanding and skills of the core area of science in the National Curriculum. The following account first presents an overview of the topic and its content, drawing particular attention to its relationship with the core area of science, and then discusses this overview with comments on approaches, organisation and merits as a worthwhile historical study.

'Images of our school' is an account of a historical project based on the children's school and immediate environment, undertaken with children aged 6–7 years. The aim of the teachers was to address the key historical concepts of time and change. Two classes in the school followed this integrated topic work for a period of one school term. The planning took account of the discernible core of history and activities formed the basis for the development of work in environmental education and science, with strong links into mathematics, language, art, movement and drama. In particular, alongside history, there was considerable emphasis on addressing knowledge, understanding and skills of the core area of science in the National Curriculum.

The project took as its central theme 'images through time', based on the premise that history at infant school level starts 'where the children are' and is concerned first with that which is within their own memory, then working back into the more distant past. It had two distinct yet interrelated parts:

1 Images of today
2 Images of the past

These were linked, with the second naturally following on from the first.

Three key subheadings (Fig. 3.1) were addressed in both parts, namely:

(a) Childhood (particularly related to school days)
(b) School buildings
(c) Games and activities

Images of today

Childhood today: images of our school day

Key concepts: Time, order and sequence

This involved an investigation into time itself, that is, sequence of time and duration of time. There was much scope at this stage for linking with

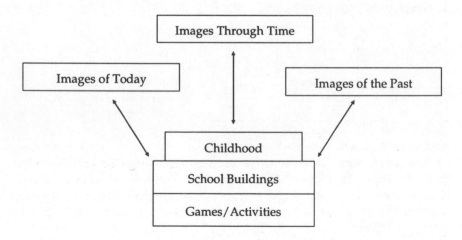

Figure 3.1 Images through time: key sub-headings

the children's work in mathematics. Various key questions were con-sidered and discussed:

- How long is a minute? an hour? a day? a week? a year?
- Why do we have clocks?
- Do we need time?
- What would happen in a world without time?

Time is indeed an extremely difficult concept to grasp. It can be described as: an interval between two events, a limited stretch of continued exist-ence, or a 'fixed' phenomenon.

A wide variety of practical activities were undertaken to help children's understanding of the concept, as discussed below.

Questions about time were then related to the school day with dis-cussion of such issues as:

- Why is it necessary to have order in our school day?
- Why is assembly always at the same time (and lunch, playtime, home-time, etc.)?
- What is a school timetable?
- What do we do in the course of a day at school (worktime, playtime, eating time, story time, etc.)?
- How long do these activities last?

Discussion was then elaborated on to include such matters as:

- What is it like to be a schoolchild today?
- What do we wear to school?
- What do we eat at school?
- What do we use at school?
- What do we bring to school?
- What time do we come to school?
- What do we have in our classrooms?
- What games do we play at playtime?
- What does our school look like?
- What is it made of?
- When was it built?
- Why is it made of these building materials?

All these issues and ideas were brought together in discussion and writing, and the key concepts of time, order and sequence were gradually linked to that of change. The children readily understood the notion that in a year, we change, and so do other things around us. As the years go by, a lot changes in our world. Fundamental questions addressed at this stage included:

- Has our school always been like this?
- Have school days always been like ours?

- Have children always played the same games and done the same activities?

And most importantly,

- How do we find out?

Practical investigations included interviews with people who went to school several or many years ago, talking to parents, grandparents, greatgrand-parents and school staff and visitors. The people interviewed were asked to comment on such matters as:

- What did they wear to school?
- What was their school building like?
- What was a school day like?
- What games did they play?

Images of the past

From this, the second major element of the project, 'Images of the past', unfolded, with its three related elements, namely

(a) School days of long ago (particularly Edwardian and Victorian times).
(b) The school building.
(c) Games and activities of long ago.

Key questions in this section were:

- What causes change?
- Will the world continue to change?
- What about the future?

Children were encouraged (with suitable help and inputs from the teachers) to think what school will be like for their own children and grandchildren – 'An imagined future school day'.

This dimension began with a major field activity, a visit to the original building of the children's present modern school – attended by many of their parents and grandparents. This original school building was replaced in 1972. The old building is now a church and the children were fascinated by its atmosphere and history.

They wrote:

The ceilings were very high in the very old Town School. In the hall I saw some very big beams and all over the hall floor were different colours of wood. All of the classrooms opened into the hall. I noticed that there were numbers on the classroom doors and the doors were all painted yellow. I went into classroom 5. It was a very big room. I saw where the coat pegs used to be. I saw steps leading up to a passage. I knew that the steps were very old because they were wearing away and they were not level. I saw that in the old school the coat pegs had one side for girls and one side for boys.

The girls had to do sewing and knitting at school for the poor boys and girls. If they didn't do enough they would have to stay in and do some more. If they had finished they would get a ticket and when they had got four tickets they would get a penny. Girls wore boots, black stockings, brown dress, blue cloak, blue and white checked apron and black straw hat with a blue ribbon. Boys wore brown cord trousers, blue jacket, black boots, white shirt and a cap.

The toilets were just two holes in the ground. The health was very bad. In 1876 the school closed because of scarlet fever. The little ones used slate and sat on benches but the older children wrote with an ink pen. They all worked in one room and their main projects were scripture, maths and English. Every now and again inspectors came to the school to see if the children were being taught properly. They had no apparatus until the last head and she decided to do something about it. She fixed some old desk together to make a kind of slide and stuck some hooks on the door. The children got caned if they were naughty.

The children came away with fascinating insights into social history with plenty of scope for creative writing, art work, health and environmental education, mathematics and dramatic role play. First hand observations were detailed and illuminating: 'I knew the steps were very old because they were wearing out, not level.' 'I noticed that the windows were so high the children couldn't see out.'

A second focal point in the study of school days of the past was a day in school devoted entirely to role play in life of Victorian times. A large amount of preparation and overwhelming support from parents ensured that 'appropriate dress' was worn and every child wholeheartedly entered into the spirit of the occasion. The atmosphere was authentic and exciting:

For a whole day we pretended that we were at school in the olden days. It was great fun. We sang hymns in the hall . . . we played with whip and top . . . we ate some bread and cheese . . . we dressed like children of long ago.

Not only was the spirit of the occasion entered into, so too was the hard work – the drill – and the abacus mathematics. The event was recorded in a variety of innovative ways including tape recording and photography. The combined impact of the fieldwork and role play served to provide enormous enthusiasm for this topic as a whole. The key concepts of time and change readily unfolded through discussion, activity, investigation and experimentation in a completely natural manner.

From the outset, this historical topic had a sound conceptual under-pinning. The teachers' clear aim was to develop the concepts of time and change, which are essential to a sense of chronology and basic historical understanding. When considering sequence and duration of time, numerous practical tasks and activities were undertaken. The children were asked to talk amongst themselves for two minutes, then to keep silent for two minutes, and to say which seemed the longer period. This activity can be extended into running/hopping for two minutes, seeing how many words you can write down in two minutes, how far you can move in two minutes, and so on, with discussion on whether two minutes seems longer or shorter depending on what you are doing. This leads to a gradual understanding of the idea that a minute is a fixed period of time, a helpful basis for looking at clocks and learning how to tell the time. A sub-topic on clocks and time could be a useful progression, developing the concept of duration of events and the concept of time being a 'fixed' phenomenon. From 'How long is a minute?' one can progress to 'How long is an hour, a week, a lifetime?' and such questions as 'How long is it since Jesus Christ lived and Bible stories were written?' 'How long since ice and snow covered our earth and no people lived here?' An infant mind will no doubt find such questions very difficult to grasp, yet sound beginnings can be made with an understanding of both duration and sequence of events. The notion of sequence can be tackled using pictures of activities that are relevant to a day in the life of an infant, which have to be put in order. Suitable pictures can be cut out of magazines or copied from books. Ask the children to discuss what they did yesterday, what they have done today, and what they are going to do tomorrow. Key vocabulary to introduce and reinforce includes

• Before/after
• Yesterday/today/tomorrow
• Night/day

In the classroom, a large chart can be made to show the events of the day in correct order, and perhaps one of the week's events showing special happenings. These basic activities will naturally lead into the intro-duction and development of time lines in history, and can be linked to the all important progression in understanding from the concept of *time* to the concept of *change* through time. Indeed, the passage of time is a major concept to be developed; the idea that change is linked to a sequence of events, that our lives go on and we change, despite clocks and calendars. Related ideas and vocabulary to introduce include

- Day and night
- Phases of the moon – the sun and stars
- Days of the week
- Days/months/years
- The notion of years AD and years BC

A great deal of work can be done on the theme of 'ourselves' and how we change through time, perhaps linked to significant events in the year such as birthdays, Christmas, holidays, starting a new class at school. Hopefully this will lead to an understanding that as time goes on, we and the world inevitably change. From the passage of one year we can progress to thinking of change through a number of years, our own lives and families change through the years, the world around us also changes as time goes by.

This case study topic certainly demonstrates how children began to build up a chronological framework, as they followed the topic's inbuilt progression from the concept of time to that of change through time. It began, in accordance with National Curriculum recommendations, in the present, and gradually worked back from the immediate memory of the children to events of the more distant past, yet ones which had a meaningful link with their families and community.

Another merit of this topic is that it had a discernible core of historical understanding whilst placing selected emphasis on other areas of the curriculum. It was well planned as a whole, and the teachers concerned expressed no guilt at failing to bring in every subject area. A good deal of science was incorporated into the topic. This was justified because in a period as long as a term, meaningful links and worthwhile progressive work could be pursued. Basic work in the other core areas continued at times other than those allocated to topic work. It is perhaps useful to highlight how the core area of science was skilfully integrated with history.

Science content

Types and uses of materials

This theme was delivered through an investigation of building materials. Questions addressed included

- What was the 'old school' built of? What is the modern school built of?
- Why have some building materials changed through time?
- Why are some building materials apparently better than others? Can we test this fact?
- What factors must be considered when choosing them (expense, durability, weather-proofing, availability, etc.)?
- What experiments can we do to investigate whether some materials are harder or tougher than others?

Materials in the classroom were also investigated:

- How have these changed since the 'old school' days?
- What is slate? Where does it come from? Why don't we use it now?
- Where does our paper come from? (Introducing ideas about conservation and limited world resources.)
- Slate/paper as surfaces. What will mark them? Clean them?
- Chalk – What is it? Where does it come from?
- What other materials are there in the classroom? (Wooden desks, plastic apparatus, metal scissors, cloth, etc.)
- Did the Victorian school have plastic apparatus?
- Did they have wooden desks?
- Group the materials in our school today according to their characteristics and origins.

Earth and atmosphere

This was approached by looking at:

- What natural materials do we find in our school building and in classroom materials – stones, chalk, sand, timber?
- Where have these come from?

The key idea was developed that all have come from the earth and that the earth's resources are limited. Weather affects natural materials (e.g. weathering of stone buildings). Evidence was sought of weathering on the school building which changes a building through time. (This is very relevant to the topic as a whole – the idea of a building not lasting for ever and the concepts of time and change.)

Electricity and magnetism

This area was delivered by posing questions for investigation such as:

- How is our school heated and lighted?
- Where does the power come from? (Leading to the key concept of energy.)
- Was this power available in Victorian times? (Introducing the idea of candle power – sources of heat and light and ideas on how these have changed through historical times.)
- What domestic appliances do we have in school today (kitchen equipment, kettles, projectors etc.)? In schools of yesterday?
- When was electricity 'invented'?

Information technology including micro-electronics

This was a very relevant theme as it obviously represents one of the key changes since Victorian/Edwardian times. Children in schools today use computers, tape recorders, television.

- What are the benefits of these?
- Why do we want to store information?

(This could help children to think about imagined future school days).

Energy

This theme was originally brought into the topic in relation to the foods eaten during the day. We need food for energy so that we can do our schoolwork, run around the playground, etc. Methods of preparing foods over the years and the nature and variety of foods eaten were also considered:

- Have schools always had kitchens?
- Did the children's grandparents have lunch at school?
- Kitchens then and now.
- Butter-making of old (they made some!).
- Have our diets changed over the years?

From food, the concept of energy was developed by looking at toys which move and use energy (clockwork toys from historical times) and then to machines which need a source of energy in order to work, and power needed to heat and light the school.

Sound and music

This was covered by investigating 'Sounds of our school today' and 'Sounds of yesterday':

- What musical instruments do we hear and use in the course of a day? Were they to be found in Victorian schools?
- Songs/hymns of Edwardian/Victorian times.
- Music of that era.
- School bells – from hand to electric.

Basic skills and approaches as to science were, of course, relevant throughout the entire topic as children were actively encouraged to

- plan,
- carry out,
- interpret results and findings,
- draw inferences, and
- communicate exploratory tasks and findings.

The children's learning in science was extensive, whilst other meaningful integration occurred with the areas of mathematics, language, drama, art and the cross-curricular themes of environmental education and health education.

To consider approaches to and organisation of the children's learning it will be apparent that a great deal of preliminary work centred around class discussion of issues and ideas relating to the concepts of time, change and sequence. As the topic as a whole developed it involved class-centred discussions and a tremendous amount of individual and small grοu̠p investigation and recording. A key question raised throughout the topic was 'how do we find out?'. This approach was totally in line with the National Curriculum's recommendations on historical enquiry and communications for Key Stage 1, which state that

> Pupils should be encouraged to ask questions about the past. They should have opportunities to communicate awareness and understanding of history orally, visually and in writing, for example: act out an episode from the past through drama or dance.
>
> (DES 1991c)

Clear links with the elements of the programme of study for Key Stage 1 were made by focusing on pictures, photographs, adults talking about the past, a building and written material as historical sources, and eye witness accounts. The pupils certainly progressed from familiar situations to those more distant in time and place. They were taught about everyday life, work, leisure and culture of men, women and children in the past, with a particular focus on education.

Links with attainment targets

All three attainment targets were adequately covered. The following summary provides a useful analysis, with examples from the topic being matched to the National Curriculum documentation. This method of analysis and recording is, of course, transferable to any topic or school theme, and provides a basis for using children's work in record-keeping.

Links with AT1

- *Use common words and phrases relating to the passing of time, for example: old, new, before, after, long ago, days of the week, months, years.*

As discussed above, a great deal of preliminary work was done on the concept of the passage of time, and all of the above suggested vocabulary was introduced and then used in the context of the practical investigations. Children's oral and written work provided a great deal of evidence of understanding of such words and phrases:

'After we get to school, we wait for the bell to ring.'

'On Monday we have a birthday assembly and after that we come back into the class.'

'I do not like it on Monday when we have to do the news.'

'On Monday, Tuesday, Wednesday, Thursday we do maths and on Friday we have PE.'

'Long ago in 1825 the first town school was built. 44 years after that it was knocked down and a new school had to be built.'

'In the olden days teachers were a lot stricter than they are now."

'Children in the days long ago were not allowed to play with toys on Sundays. Mondays, Tuesdays, Wednesdays, Thursdays, Fridays, Saturdays they played and on Sundays they went to church. That was years ago.'

- *Identify a sequence of events and talk about why they happened, for example: changes in the life of a pupil's family.*

This strand was well covered by talking with pupils, parents, grand-parents and other visitors about how school days and related aspects had changed through time. Input was also provided by one of the teachers and her own family; she and her daughter provided very different accounts of 'a day at school' in their own childhood. Illustrated timelines were built up to show events in sequence, and this, of course, provided excellent reinforcement for the underpinning aim of teaching the concept of change through time.

'When my teacher went to school it was not like it is now. They had to be really good or they got the cane. They spent ages all day doing maths and writing. PE was like drill and they had to stand outside in rows.'

'My teacher's daughter went to a school and she got smacked with a ruler just because she didn't draw a margin straight. She wore a brown skirt and a brown cap and brown knickers. She did much more PE and games than my teacher did.'

- *Observe differences between ways of life at different times in the past, for example: the clothes worn in different periods.*

This strand was a major focus of study, highlighted on the Victorian school day. Much attention was paid to appropriate dress for the occasion, and stories and pictures were used as sources to investigate the clothing that would have been worn by children at the 'old Town School'.

'Well a lot of very poor children came to the school and if they came to the school regularly then they would get some of the clothing that the girls used to knit and sew. If they were away from school for no good reason then their mum or dad would have to pay a fine. The girls uniform was brown dresses with blue and white checked pinafores over them, black stockings, big boots and a black straw hat with a blue ribbon round it.'

'Girls had to do all the knitting and sewing. Their dinners were prob-ably cabbage and stodge. I'm glad our school isn't like this now. Our school is a happy school.'

'When I go to school I wear a navy blue jumper, black trousers and a blue T-shirt or a track suit. The girls wear a light blue and white checked skirt. Some of the girls wear silver petticoats. It wasn't like this when they went to school in Victorian days.'

Links with AT2

• *Develop awareness of different ways of representing past events, for example: pictures, written accounts, films, television programmes, plays, songs, reproductions of objects, museum displays.*
• *Distinguish between different versions of events, for example: different accounts by pupils of events which happened in the school a week, a month, a year ago.*

The children were encouraged to draw on a wide range of sources that involved understanding of their school in the past. A great deal of oral history was used, as well as TV programmes, objects and written accounts. Combined with field notes, sketches, photographs and tape recordings, these provided a sound basis for historical understanding. Effort was also made to record field experiences and role play observations in a wide variety of ways – factual and creative accounts were written and shared, photographs were displayed, sketches drawn and mathematical data represented pictorially. The teachers skilfully encouraged the sharing of opinions and conclusions of investigations by providing wide-ranging opportunities for oral, pictorial and written communication. Children's shared thoughts ranged from discovered facts to personal and reflective opinion, encouraging an understanding of different ways of thinking and representing past events.

'Isn't time a funny thing, Miss? It's a bit like a dream . . . . You can't see it or feel it, it's just there'.

Links with AT3

• *Find out about the past from different types of historical source, for example: historical houses, objects in museums, paintings, photographs, coins, newspapers.*

Once again, this attainment target was well covered and aimed to help pupils develop skills in using sources. At Key Stage 1, it is appropriate for learners to begin to appreciate that questions we want to answer about the past can often be resolved by using sources of a variety of kinds. In particular, these children were encouraged to ask questions and seek answers from the sources they were investigating. They were also encouraged to use evidence from sources and to tell others, to communicate their historical understanding.

'The windows look so high, the children couldn't look out of them. Was that so they didn't stop working?'

'Why was there a coal fire in every classroom? The caretaker probably had to put a bucket of coal in front of the fire.'

'We played with a whip and top and sang hymns and heard God stories. It was fun at school in the olden days.'

'I saw some bits of wood. I think they were part of ceiling beams. Some of the bricks were different than the others. I wonder why.'

A concluding summary relating to this particular topic, should highlight its merits which will hopefully be reflected by any school planning on integrated historical study. The topic was, of course, evaluated by the teachers concerned. Whilst space does not allow for a full critique, inevitably, in hindsight, some changes could have been made. The following represents a useful checklist of the topic's merits:

- It had clear aims, stated both in a conceptual underpinning and plan of content and purposes for learning derived mainly from the content of history but also from other areas of the curriculum.
- It identified only those other areas of the curriculum with which useful and meaningful integration could be achieved. It did not attempt to 'drag in' every curriculum subject and theme. Furthermore, the discernible and worthwhile core of history was respected throughout.
- It made meaningful links between the attainment targets and programmes of study for history, and provided sound coverage of both of these elements.
- Statements of attainment were used as guidelines to assist in the planning of specific tasks. Often tasks were devised which were related to a number of levels, and covered more than one attainment target.
- It took account of general requirements of the programme of study for Key Stage 1, including links between other subjects, as already mentioned, information technology capability, cross-curricular themes and provision for learners with special educational needs.
- Teacher observations and examples of children's writing and other work were used as an ongoing element of recording and assessment throughout the topic.
- A good variety of teaching methods were used, including story telling and other presentations led by the teacher, discussion, fieldwork with individual and group investigations, experimentation, use of role play and drama, use of TV, museum objects, radio, tapes and other secondary resource materials.
- A key element of the topic focused on the pupils' own enquiry and communication of historical knowledge and understanding.

OBJECTS AND ARTEFACTS

Before proceeding with a more general discussion on planning in Key Stage 1, a little more attention will now be paid to the use of objects and artefacts as historic sources. These were an integral part of the case study described above, and are certainly a most important form of evidence about the past. In many ways, the use of real objects follows on from and complements the telling of stories. Stories 'told by teacher' must be taken on trust by young learners. Real objects, on the other hand, add a new dimension to learning. They introduce the concrete – the down to earth existence – which will sit alongside imaginative representation in children's minds. In terms of skills progression, real objects are useful at any stage, though perhaps are more so with children who have been in school for two or three terms, who are more accomplished in reading, writing and other learning and recording skills. It will be useful for any teacher of history to make a personal collection of a range and variety of artefacts and resources that can be supplemented at appropriate times with those borrowed from friends, relatives, museums, or the children themselves. The scope is endless and may include:

- Photographs (of self as a baby, growing up, adult, family, home, possessions, holidays, etc.)
- Clothes (of days gone by)
- Coins (especially those now no longer in use – predecimal money and coins from earlier times)
- Household objects (of historic interest, perhaps handed down by parents and grandparents)
- Newspapers (facsimile reproductions are available, but it is not too late to save papers telling of key local, national and world events of today – in a year, five years, ten years time, they will be valuable artefacts)
- Books (of your childhood and those handed down from previous generations, old school log books, etc.)
- Toys and games (also those of parents and grandparents)
- Music (tapes and records of songs of your childhood and teenage years, and indeed adult life)
- Miscellaneous items – wartime ration books, transport or theatre tickets, price tags, advertisements, holiday brochures, soldiers' uniforms, etc.

Of course, a major distinction must be made when considering objects and artefacts between those which can be used by the young learners themselves, and those which are useful source material for planning tasks. There is a place for both, supplemented with library, museum and record/archive offices resources. Key issues to bear in mind when making a collection of objects for the children to use are as follows:

- They should be well preserved and not too fragile – learners will be anxious to handle them/use them, and they should be in a state that can be thoroughly investigated without leading to destruction.
- They should have clear and identifiable links with people, that is, they should be artefacts of social history. Where possible, it is a good idea to

have a collection that represents as many different members of the family as possible (baby, teenager, grandfather, uncle the soldier, auntie the foreign traveller, etc.).

- It is a good idea to make a collection which represents a specific period of time or event in history, for example, school in Victorian times, World War II objects, life of the 1960s, etc.
- It is especially beneficial to have objects that can be compared with similar things of the present age (the flat iron and electric iron, washing dolly with modern machines, etc.). Comparisons of this kind develop important historical skills and ideas of 'what it was like then' and 'what it is like now'. Linked to this is, of course, the all-important consideration that some things have not changed over a period of time.

Further general issues to consider involve storage, display and care of historic objects. A temporary classroom museum is an excellent idea, and display and storage should be given very serious attention, definitely involving the children themselves. One could usefully discuss, for example, whether it is appropriate to keep old and perhaps beautiful objects in a modern plastic storage box or suitcase. How and where can they be kept safely and displayed to best advantage? This will lead to the all-important issue of responsibility – and the idea of the children as caretakers of valuable objects. Attitudes and values are vital elements of this procedure, and one would hopefully expect young people to care for historic material in the same positive and concerned way that they would care for an animal or plant in the classroom. It is important to stress such things as respect for the past, the need to care for borrowed belongings, preservation of valuable materials, and concern for future generations, that they too can have the benefit of the things we are learning from. Key questions to consider are:

- How will the children be involved in displaying, labelling, caretaking?
- How will safety be ensured (both of the objects and of the children!)?
- How and when will the children handle/play with/investigate the objects?
- Who will contribute to the display?

In an ideal world the answer to the final question will, of course, be both teacher and children, with additions from a museum education service or other people. No doubt the teacher will need to stimulate interest and begin the classroom collection, encouraging the children to bring in their own objects, photographs, etc., having talked with parents, grandparents and friends.

Gradually, an awareness of people long ago is built up, through objects and artefacts from a past of which the children have no direct experience. Activities such as handling objects, drawing them, asking questions about them, discussing them, all lead naturally into further enquiries about family history. The social/human dimension is a vital component of this, and indeed, no discussion on collections of useful resources would be complete without further emphasis being placed on the use of people themselves.

- *Make tape recordings of people.* Start your own collection now that will be invaluable in a few years' time. Interview your own parents, grand-parents, elderly friends, neighbours and senior citizens of the community about life in their own childhood days. Interview young people now (tales told on tape by children and teenagers of today about their lives, games, school days, food and clothing, etc., will make fascinating listening in the future).
- *Use people themselves.* Ask elderly relatives or friends to come into the classroom and talk with the children about their experiences of historic times. With Key Stage 1 children, this activity will need to be carefully structured, as attention span will inevitably be very limited. Brief your visitors well, and plan a series of suitable interview questions ahead of time with the children. This will probably lead to a far more productive visit than 'uncensored tales' by the visitor.
- Remember also that you are an artefact in your own right and one well qualified to talk in a structured way about childhood experiences and family recollections. Even the youngest teacher will be a worthwhile resource – yesterday is past history to a young mind. Indeed, stories of your own life will make a very valuable contribution to time lines and sequence of the past. Bear in mind the true story of a headteacher in a County Durham infant school who was asked if she was around in the days when dinosaurs roamed the earth!

Use opportunities with people and artefacts to reinforce the basic voca-bulary of the chronology of time: 'then', 'now', 'long ago', 'during my life-time', 'before', 'afterwards', 'days/years of the past', 'today/yesterday/tomorrow'.

It is also helpful to formulate a series of questions designed to help with the interpretation of artefacts as historic evidence, to include:

- What is it?
- What is it made of?
- Does it have a smell/make a sound?
- What colour is it?
- Is it natural or made by people?
- Is it worn?
- What was it used for?
- Has the use changed?
- Who made it?

- Why was it made?
- What is it worth?
- What does it tell us about life in the past?
- What does it tell us about people in the past?
- Do we use anything like it today?
- If not, why not?

Do consider at length, the possibilities of deriving the best possible use out of objects, photographs and people in the classroom. Whilst it is very difficult to generalise, key issues to consider are: how could they be used as starting points, what range of topics might be developed from them, and what will be their ongoing use to ensure continuity and progression in the acquisition of historical knowledge, understanding and skills?

PLANNING AND RESOURCES – THE WAY FORWARD

No sound history will occur at any stage without adequate planning. This will be at the levels of planning the curriculum as a whole and of planning particular schemes of work and topics for the study unit. A curriculum plan for history in Key Stage 1 is an essential starting point for the school, and *Non-Statutory Guidance* provides a useful checklist of things to include in this:

- aims and objectives;
- order in which study units should be taught;
- curriculum plans for each year group;
- provision for pupils at different levels of attainment, including those with special educational needs;
- links with other subjects and crosscurricular elements including equal opportunities;
- resources to be used;
- teaching methods;
- methods of assessment and recordkeeping;
- a scheme of work for each study unit;
- arrangements for monitoring and review.

(NCC 1991a)

Schemes of work, developed through topics will no doubt cover a variety of subject areas, and as already stressed, very careful planning is needed to ensure that the history component is a coherent, progressive whole. It is helpful to tease out ways in which this history will be linked to other subject areas apart from in content. For example, the use of stories, fieldwork investigations and information databases can all be developed in a cross-curricular way to address specific programmes of study and attainment targets of other subjects – a far more satisfactory situation than rather vague connections with every other aspect of the curriculum. Key decisions clearly have to be made in terms of both selection of topics and how to develop work across years 1 and 2. It is important for these two facets of planning to be discussed together when school and class approaches to the study unit are being decided. If very general topics are being pursued, such as 'Myself', 'Toys', 'Holidays', 'Our school', 'Where I live', etc., then the historical component will need to be thought through carefully so that there is plenty of scope for appropriate activities and investigation using evidence from the past. *Non-Statutory Guidance* (NCC 1991a) provides a useful outline plan of such general themes, with suggestions for historic content in the first three years in school. Detailed attention need be paid to:

- *Activities* which foster skills of historical enquiry and communication, and which cover all three attainment targets, whilst meeting the individual needs of all of the learners.
- *Assessment and recording* arrangements, which can be related to the range of tasks and activities identified, taking account of oral work and children's written and illustrative material.
- *Key questions* to be raised throughout the topic which will guide progressive historic enquiry.
- *Cross-curricular links* with other core and foundation subjects refer- ring to specific programmes of study and attainment targets; also to cross-curricular skills, themes and dimensions.
- *Resources* (discussed below).

Given that it is not necessary to teach all of the elements of the programme of study in any one year, attention must be paid to ways of developing work across the years, bearing in mind pupils' individual needs and attainment levels. Again, it is extremely difficult to generalise, but in reception class and, indeed in year 1, historical understanding can only grow from a child's personal experience and immediate situation. Reception children could well be asked to think about themselves, their own lives (days of the week, birthdays, special events, how they must take care of themselves in order to 'grow and change') and people and homes in their neighbourhood. 'Where I live', 'What I play with', 'My journey to school', 'What I eat', 'My friends', 'Special days', 'What I like to wear', 'People in school/at home' are all good starting points. Through year 1, the work on pupils' own life situations and immediate family can be developed into the children's own past, introducing basic vocabulary on the chronology of time. Stories will be particularly important at this stage, including picture books of the past, folk tales, teachers' own tales of the past, myths and legends. Stories combined with illustrations will make a powerful combination of sources for helping children to link events and people with the written and spoken word. Photographs and artefacts can similarly be used in year 1, with an emphasis on discussion, observation and sequencing. As discussed above, these will be of enormous benefit in terms of developing techniques of questioning and considering evidence.

Year 2 is probably the appropriate time to broaden the sense of past and develop a chronological framework, by going back to other generations remembered within the children's families, and then on to the even more distant past. Stories, interviews, artefacts, illustrations and various form of written evidence will be necessary for the task. Careful selection of stories and other material should aim to help children distinguish between fact, fiction and imagination. The study of national or world events, or the lives of famous people are good ways of broadening the scope of topics. Adequate attention should be paid to developing schemes and specific activities which help to lead naturally into the order of study units which has been arranged for year 2 children when they proceed into Key Stage 2.

Without doubt, planning and implementation of successful schemes and topics will have implications for resources. Integrated themes will be taught by using stories of various kinds, periods and cultures; artefacts; photographs; painting and other illustrations; written sources; interviews; music and opportunities for studying buildings/sites through fieldwork.

The above section on the use of objects and artefacts will hopefully give encouragement for every teacher's personal collection of resources. Many historic objects and photographs can be acquired at little or no cost – a visit to a jumble sale or an elderly relative's attic may provide a wealth of useful things. Many of us regret not having taken advantage of lost opportunities to acquire items long since given away. The following table will serve as a useful checklist for schools building up a resource collection for the teaching of history.

People
- Recorded interviews with friends, relatives, people in the community.
- List of names of people willing to come and talk with the children about historical events.
- Names of local 'experts' to contact, e.g. local history librarian, education officer of museum, officer in charge of planning office.

Photographs
- Of people, homes, holidays, the locality, well-known events, the school through time (build up your own collection of the school).

Books
- Stories of various periods and cultures.
- Reference books, folk tales, myths and legends.
- Works about the lives of well-known people, key events etc., published scheme books.

Written sources
- These will need very careful selection for Key Stage 1 children but may include: parish records, maps, legal documents, manuscripts, personal records (letters, diaries, wills), school log books, archival sources and packs.

Mechanical
- Tape recordings, videos, TV and radio programmes, slides, cameras, microcomputers and relevant software.

Other illustrative material
- Posters, pictures, paintings, portraits, cartoons.

Music
- Records, tapes, song words, scores of different periods.

Objects
- Clothing, coins, household goods, event-specific items, e.g. gas mask, ration book, toys, recipes, tickets.

Outside school
- Publications lists and educational packs from museums, sites of historic interest, historic houses, National Trust properties, etc.
- Details of houses/museums/sites open for school visits.
- Maps of the neighbourhood with suggestions for places of historic interest.
- List of places where it is possible to do brass rubbings/find out about archaeology.
- Details of the Parish Church – name of Vicar and information about when school parties are able to make a study.
- List of places where it is possible to see or take part in historical reconstruction – music/drama/role play from the past.

The need for assessment and methods of gathering evidence of attainment is discussed in other parts of this book set aside for this purpose, but it must be emphasised that as far as history is concerned, understanding the relationship between the attainment targets and programmes of study is crucial. Children can only cover the attainment targets through the historical content of the appropriate programme of study and attainment targets and statements of attainment will guide the planning of activities and monitoring of progress and achievement. Evidence of attainment in history will be collected in a variety of ways, including observation of work, talking with and questioning individuals and groups, and discussing writing, illustrations and other materials produced by the children. It will be helpful to record activities, details of questions and concepts under consideration, and the range of attainment targets/statements of attainment targeted, as well as the results.

In conclusion, it is hoped that the case study and general discussion provided within this chapter have shown that it is indeed possible to incorporate sound history teaching into the topic-based approach to learning. The initial choice of topics is vital – allowing scope for progression and development throughout the school. Effective planning will take account of the discernible historical core related to the programmes of study and attainment targets for history and also related to cross-curricular links. Of course, there is need for sequence, development, progression and structure to ensure that children are learning about change, about chronological framework, and about people in the context of past societies. We hope also, that in making their plans, teachers will ensure that excitement and imagination are not left out of this rather academic sounding formula. The best infant history must surely be about preparing young learners to have a genuine interest in the past outside of themselves and helping them to enjoy it.

Chapter 4

Science and topic work

APPROACHES TO LEARNING

It is the purpose of this chapter to illuminate and discuss how the National Curriculum for science might be implemented in infant classrooms in a way that both promotes and extends good practice in topic work. Central to the National Curriculum Order for Science is the notion that a broad, balanced and meaningful science education is a basic entitlement for all children. Central to this chapter is the notion that this is readily achieved when a range of learning processes are understood and engaged.

There is probably no better way to start than by 'visiting' a number of infant classrooms. Consider the following scenarios and 'snatches' of conversation taking place within them.

Reception

A group of reception class children are engrossed in the classroom's play house. In their world of domestic role play it is seven o'clock in the morning. Dolls wake up and are washed and dressed. In actual fact some are washed and then dressed, others are dressed and then washed. The table is set for breakfast – involving the selection of appropriate cutlery and the required amount. Spoons for cereal and sugar, knives for toast, plates, bowls, cups and saucers are organised and placed on the table. After breakfast, the washing up is done and then the house itself needs to be cleaned. Dusters, brooms, sponges and water are all considered necessary for the latter task. Next it is time to wash the dolls' clothes, raising the interesting questions of where would be the best place to dry them, and how long they will take to dry. One by one the jobs are done. In all, a lengthy and complex series of household tasks is accomplished.

Anne: Seven o'clock. Time to get up.
John: We wake up early at our house. Every morning.
Susan: So do we.
John: Daddy says we should thank my baby brother for that.

Susan: My daddy gets washed and dressed first.

John: Why?

Susan: So he can bring mummy a cup of tea in bed. Then he goes off to work to earn some money.

Cheryl: What does mummy do?

Susan: She drinks her tea, then she gets us up.

Anne: Let's get our children up.

John: Can I join in?

Anne: No – you've gone to work, like daddy.

John: That's not fair – I want to help.

Cheryl: My mummy lets my daddy help. All the time. Even when he doesn't want to.

Susan: Come on, then. Time to wake the children up.

Anne: Wake up, Emma. Wake up, Jane. You too, Andrew.

Cheryl: It's no use hiding under the blanket, Lisa. I can see you.

Susan: Time you all got ready for breakfast.

Cheryl: I'll wash Emma and Lisa.

Susan: And I'll wash Andrew and Jane.

Cheryl: We can't do them all at once. The sink isn't big enough.

John: Susan, why don't you wash your two while Cheryl gets hers dressed?

Cheryl: I can't wash them when they're dressed.

John: Why not?

Anne: Their clothes'll be in the way, silly.

Susan: And they'll get all wet.

John: You always get wet when you have a wash.

Anne: Not the children – their clothes.

Cheryl: You can't wash anybody properly like that.

Anne: How can you clean your skin when it's all covered up?

John: My daddy washes with his clothes on.

Anne: Yuk!

John: Well, in his vest, anyway.

Susan: That's not like having all your clothes on.

Cheryl: No. There's enough of him showing to give his neck a good wash.

Anne: And behind his ears.

Cheryl: And his hands and face.

John: So we could wash the children with some of their clothes on.

Susan: I suppose so. We can try anyway.

John: I don't like having a wash.

Cheryl: You should have one every day.

John: Why?

Susan: Cos boys grow more dirt than girls.

Susan and Cheryl begin washing and dressing the dolls.

Anne: We'll lay the table for breakfast. Come on, John.
John: What do we need?
Anne: Some knives, forks and spoons. And some dishes and some plates. And cups and saucers.
John: I'll set the places.
Anne: One for Lisa, one for Andrew, one for Emma and one for Jane.
John: What's for breakfast?
Anne: Cornflakes first, then eggs and bacon. And a cup of tea, so don't forget the tea pot and the sugar bowl.
John: Any toast? I like toast.
Anne: Get the toaster out then.
John: We'll need some bread.
Anne: And the mumar . . . the marlamu . . . mumalar . . .
John: And the paper.
Anne: The what?
John: The paper. My daddy always reads the paper while he's having his breakfast.
Anne: Does he?

Breakfast is served and eaten.

Susan: Time to do the washing up.
Anne: We'll do that while you and Cheryl take the children to school.
Cheryl: Come on, children. Put your coats on – time for school.
Susan: Hurry. We don't want to be late.
John: Do we have to wash up?
Anne: Yes. Put the dirty dishes in the sink. I'll wash and you wipe.
John: Posh people have a dishwasher.
Anne: We're not posh. As soon as Susan and Cheryl get back, we'll have some housework to do.
John: More work?
Anne: Yes. There are floors to mop and windows to clean, and lots of dusting and polishing too. We've got to wash the children's clothes and dry them too.
John: Will it take long?
Anne: Not if we all help.

Year 1/2

A class of middle infant children pursue their topic on trees. The glorious golden bronze and amber shades of autumn leaves brighten the grey surfaces of the table tops. One group of children has collected a number of horse chestnut leaves, recently fallen from the tree. A lively discussion takes place about the shapes of these leaves and the interesting colour patterns which can be seen in them. Close observation reveals that the edges of the leaves tend to be brown and brittle whilst the interior veins retain their deep green colour. This pattern seems to be shared by almost all of the leaves that the group has collected. The children try to see if it is possible to put their leaves into order or sequence, ranging from the leaf with the largest amount of chlorophyll ('green') left in it, to that which has the least. Two leaves have only a small amount of chlorophyll left. In both cases it follows the line of the central vein of the leaf, and the surrounding areas are brownish yellow, brittle and crumbling.

Ramjit: Look how many leaves we've collected, miss.
Cameljit: What sort of leaves are they?
Asaf: I've found a picture of them in this book.
Teacher: Yes, there they are. Those are horse chestnut leaves.
Sukinder: They're a funny shape, aren't they, miss? Not like ordinary leaves.
Asaf: More like lots of little leaves stuck together.
Ramjit: The ones at the top are longer than the ones nearest the stem.
Cameljit: Look at all the sharp edges on them.
Ramjit: Like tiny teeth, aren't they?
Sukinder: And they've all got little lines in them.
Asaf: My granny's hands are like that. They've got blue lines on the back.
Cameljit: Everybody's hands have.
Teacher: That's right. They're called veins.
Cameljit: Veins? What are they for?
Teacher: Well, in people they help to carry blood round the body.
Asaf: But trees don't have blood. What do they need veins for?
Teacher: To carry goodness through the leaves. This helps them to grow healthy and strong. The colour of the leaves tells you how healthy they are.
Sukinder: So green means they're healthy.
Teacher: Yes.
Ramjit: But these leaves aren't green all over. Look.
Cameljit: They are. Well, they're green in the middle, anyway.
Sukinder: Where the veins are.
Ramjit: But not on the edges. See, they're going brown.
Asaf: Brown and yellowy.
Ramjit: And crinkly.
Ramjit: And bits are coming off.
Sukinder: Miss, he's broken it!
Teacher: Don't worry, there are plenty of leaves left.
Cameljit: And they all look the same as that one.

Sukinder: See, they're green on the inside and brown on the outside.
Ramjit: That leaf must be older than the other one.
Cameljit: How can you tell?
Ramjit: It's got more brown in it.
Sukinder: So has this one. And this one.
Asaf: This one's got lots of green still left.
Teacher: Let's see if we can sort them out. Let's put the greenest leaves
            on this side of the table, and all the browner leaves on that side.
Asaf: All our leaves have got some green and brown in them.
Ramjit: Perhaps the brown comes in autumn and makes the leaves fall
            off the trees.
Sukinder: Do all leaves go brown like these, miss?
Teacher: That's a good question. Perhaps we could try to find out when
            we've finished sorting these horse chestnut leaves.

The children spend some time sorting the leaves.

Ramjit: These two leaves have hardly any green left in them. Look.
            There's just a bit left.
Asaf: Where?
Sukinder: There, see? Along the middle of the leaf.
Cameljit: Where the middle vein is.
Ramjit: It's the same on this leaf too.
Cameljit: The rest of the leaf is all brown and crackly.
Sukinder: It looks old and crumbly on the outside.
Ramjit: But there's some life left on the inside.

Year 2/3

Top infant children are standing in a group, gathered round a plastic
bucket suspended from the ceiling girder. The bucket rests some 20 cm
from the floor, secured to a ceiling hook by means of a thin nylon string.
Beakers of damp sand are gradually added to the bucket. The number of
beakers emptied in this way is duly recorded. Eventually the process is
halted and delight registers on the children's faces when the string breaks
and the bucket crashes to the floor. The next phase of the investigation
continues with the re-erection of the empty bucket attached to a new
string of identical length but different variety.

We witness an investigation into fair testing of the strengths or
breaking strains of different strings – cotton, sisal and synthetic – in a
range of thicknesses, but of standardised length.

Peter: More sand, Kevin.
Kevin: How many beakers is that?
Wendy: Nine, so far.

Janet:	Here's another one.
Peter:	Tip it in the bucket, then.
Linda:	Ten . . .
Kevin:	Keep filling the beakers, Simon.
Janet:	The bucket's nearly full.
Peter:	No sign of the string breaking yet.
Linda:	Eleven . . .
Wendy:	Twelve . . .
Kevin:	That bucket must be getting heavy by now.
Janet:	Thirteen . . .
Wendy:	Fourteen . . .
Peter:	Watch out – there it goes!
Kevin:	Miss, the string's snapped.
Teacher:	Good. Did you count the number of beakers it took to fill the bucket?
Wendy:	Yes, miss. It was fourteen.
Teacher:	Fine. Pick the bucket up, and empty it out. Don't forget to write fourteen alongside nylon.
Peter:	Done it, miss.
Teacher:	Let's test another kind of string.
Kevin:	Yes. What about this thin one.
Linda:	That's cotton.
Kevin:	Will you tie it up for us, miss?
Teacher:	Yes,
Kevin:	How much cotton do we need?
Wendy:	About this much.
Peter:	That's not fair.
Wendy:	Why not?
Kevin:	It won't be big enough.
Teacher:	How can we make the test fair?
Peter:	Look at the nylon string, that's much longer than the cotton.
Kevin:	The second piece ought to be as long as the first one.
Peter:	It won't be fair unless they're both the same size. Will it miss?
Kevin:	We should measure the nylon string first . . .
Peter:	And then make all the other strings just as long.
Kevin:	Yes. We can't find out which is the strongest if some are short and some are long.
Peter:	They've all got to be the same.

These three case studies describe and illuminate situations in which children's natural processes of learning are engaged. Science is being learnt within their own familiar environment. The knowledge, understanding and processes of science are developed in the context of pupils' individual potential and natural curiosity. In each case the teacher acts as facilitator, enabler and indeed director of this development. Analysis of the conversation taking place in reception class leaves us with little doubt that the children are building upon natural experiences which they automatically bring to the classroom. These experiences are developed through a range of activities that are set out, in which the children may engage themselves. The teacher is, of course, aware that science will develop from the situation, observes the scene regularly and intervenes when she considers it appropriate to do so in order to guide thinking. During this 'pretend' day, key concepts such as order and sequence are discovered, discussed and seen to have importance, albeit in an imaginative situation. For example order and sequence of dressing and washing and of washing and drying are noticed and logically reasoned. The need for selection of materials is also essential to the discussion, such as the appropriate cutlery and crockery for eating certain foods and the choice of suitable cleaning devices for doing the best job with the house. At the end of the activity, a lengthy and complex series of tasks has been accomplished, introducing and reinforcing a sound scientific approach and knowledge and skills that are appropriate for the children's stage of conceptual development.

In year 1/2, organisation is through a topic which clearly has science as the central core. It is not difficult to identify and extract the science content, yet it is apparent that other areas of the curriculum arise from this core (e.g. what wonderful language and art work may derive from 'the glorious golden bronze and amber shades of autumn leaves' on the 'grey surfaces of the table tops'). Skills of detailed observation and investigation are essential to the task being undertaken. Patterns are recognised, the concepts of order and sequence are considered and indeed the task invites further investigation. Do all horse chestnut leaves lose their chlorophyll in a similar pattern? What about leaves from other varieties of trees? Once again, the children's natural capacity for learning is engaged using familiar objects from the world around them, yet the teacher's role is crucial in furthering their knowledge of science. The learners demonstrate a capacity to make connections, to discover and to test their own ideas, arguments and discoveries. In this particular classroom, experience is organised through a topic with obvious scientific content.

Finally, year 2/3 demonstrates a situation in which the children's experience and learning is organised according to the subject matter of science itself. Experiments are taking place to investigate the strengths or breaking strains of different strings. Underpinning this is the development of the key concept of fair testing. As in the other two scenarios, the teacher's role is critical in the development of the concepts of science through the children's own investigations and experimentation. Learning is dependent upon the organisation of experience, upon making connections and discoveries, and logical testing of these experiences. It is therefore an organised event, dependent upon natural processes. The activities in which the children are engaged demand the successful use of these processes. In part, the teacher's role involves providing ways of introducing children to and enabling them to use such strategies. In each of the three case studies, this is successfully achieved, resulting in 'good infant practice' in science education. Of course, one could argue that these three examples have no obvious connection with integrated topic work. The point being emphasised is that they demonstrate different ways of approaching the complexity of learning in early years science and that all three approaches can be incorporated into integrated work.

THE NATIONAL CURRICULUM

To return to the opening statement of this chapter, it must be stressed that much of the National Curriculum was 'put together' and based on examples of good practice. Where this exists in schools, it must be built upon, using the Orders as a useful framework. We have indeed a framework and not a syllabus.

Perhaps it should be explained here that no attempt is made within this chapter to explain in detail the specific content of science in the National Curriculum or its interpretation. The majority of readers will already be familiar with this. This book as a whole is far more concerned with approaches to teaching and learning than with specifics of content. Nevertheless, an overview of the rationale of the National Curriculum Order is provided, largely for the benefit of those beginning a career in science education and for overseas readers.

The view of science in schools embodied in the National Curriculum is that it should be an essential part of a whole curriculum that is broad, balanced, relevant and differentiated. It should be directed towards effective learning, which means ensuring that all children are eager to participate in science and are stimulated by interest and curiosity. In so doing, they should acquire scientific knowledge and understanding, develop skills of investigation and experimentation and have opportunities for communication about science. Within the framework of the National Curriculum, the teacher's role is seen partly as that of enabler, who may interact with pupils, pose questions, provide appropriate challenges and experiences and offer the children possibilities for new ways of thinking. The child's role is that of scientist in so far as understanding of the world is developed both by existing ideas that are available and by processes by which these ideas are used and then tested in new situations. Children's early experiences of the world are of vital importance. Through these experiences they continually develop ideas which enable them to make increasing sense of their environment and of the interrelationships that exist among things and happenings within it. One of the key aims of science education is to adapt or modify these original ideas to give them more explanatory power. The ideas of young children can be essentially scientific in so far as they fit the available evidence. They will, to a large extent, be limited to concrete, observable features. A child's knowledge and understanding of scientific ideas and ability for problem-solving will progressively increase as new experiences with objects and events are encountered and as skills of investigation and exploration are mastered and developed.

Alongside the gaining of knowledge and understanding, and the development of skills of scientific exploration, the National Curriculum recognises that children's attitudes are also important for learning in science. In particular, the attitudes of curiosity, respect for evidence, willingness to tolerate uncertainty, critical reflection, perseverance, open-mindedness, sensitivity to the living and non-living environment and co-operation with others are seen as being of great significance. All can be encouraged to develop in children through example and recognition, leading to higher levels of motivation and an increased willingness to participate in exploration and learning.

In summary then, the National Curriculum for science sees the teacher's role as encouraging pupils to explore and investigate their environment in an active, participatory manner and to devise learning tasks which build upon such experience. At the same time there should be wide-ranging opportunities provided for interaction with objects and both living and non-living materials. Exploration and investigation underpin the entire content, with children encouraged to pose questions, formulate hypotheses, make predictions, design and carry out investigations and experiments, interpret the results of exploration and observations and communicate these findings to others. With regard to the latter point, it should be stressed that language development goes along-side the effectiveness of learning as much in science as in other curriculum areas. Inevitably, scientific ideas will be developed and extended as a result of verbal as well as written or pictorial presentation. For this reason, the importance of working in groups as well as indivi-dually cannot be overemphasised. Communication should be with both fellow learners and with adults and should involve discussion, reflective thought, the sharing of informal ideas, and the encouragement of originality as well as more formal methods and techniques.

A key question in the mind of every early years teacher and head-teacher must be how to operationalise the structure and content of the National Curriculum for science and its related assessment procedures in order to maximise the benefit of and build upon existing good quality practice of integrated work in early years classrooms. It is a purpose of this chapter to suggest that perhaps this is not such a daunting task as it may appear. Analysis of typical classroom learning experiences may demonstrate coverage of a wide range of science statements of attainment. Indeed, it was evident in each of the three classroom scenes described earlier in this chapter that apart from knowledge and understanding of science, there was ample evidence of exploration of science – the children were actively engaged in:

• planning, hypothesising and predicting;
• designing and carrying out investigations;
• interpreting results and findings;
• drawing inferences; and
• communicating exploratory tasks and experiments.

Each represented an example of the National Curriculum, expressed in good practice.

A CASE STUDY

Attention is now turned to another case study, which is designed to elaborate on issues relating to the particular use of the topic work approach to early years science education. The topic title is 'For lunch today'. It was undertaken with a class of thirty year 1 children for a period of seven school weeks. During this time, the topic occupied a substantial proportion (over half) of the children's timetable. The aim of the topic was to develop basic knowledge, understanding, skills, concepts and attitudes of science education whilst relating these to other appropriate curriculum areas. From a starting point of 'school lunch' the children worked as a class, individually and in groups pursuing various questions and issues arising from this practical beginning.

Preliminary work leading up to the introduction of the topic's central theme involved discussion about what the children liked to eat and the sorts of food which they ate at home. Skilfully, the children's background experience of the world was given heightened awareness and used to stimulate natural interest and curiosity in food prepared at school. The key starting point for development of learning experiences was the lunch which the children ate on one particular school day. On the day in question, careful note was taken of the school main course menu: fish fingers and salad, or lamb, cabbage and potatoes. Other children ate sandwiches brought from home. From this starting point, considerable discussion took place and a series of questions were posed for possible investigation (Fig. 4.1).

The teacher's plan at the outset was sufficiently detailed to provide scope for coverage of a great deal of the National Curriculum for science relating to various attainment targets. Within this planned framework, there lay considerable scope for flexibility, for spontaneous activity and for following up the enthusiasms and interests of the children concerned.

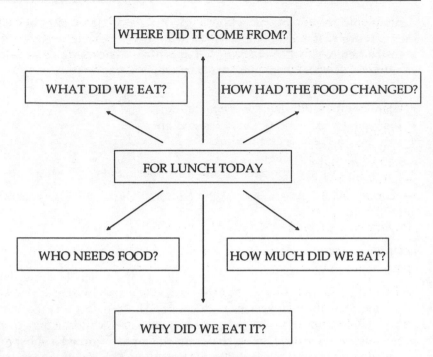

Figure 4.1 For lunch today: questions for investigation

Preplanning[2]

Plan at the outset for a topic on 'for lunch today'[3]

The National Curriculum 5–16
Programmes of study: for Key Stage 1, 5–7-year-olds.
Both profile components of science will be developed throughout the topic, namely:

- Profile component 1: Exploration of science
- Profile component 2: Knowledge and understanding of science

Also, pupils will actively be developing and using a variety of skills and techniques of communication and developing an understanding of science in everyday life.

Profile component 1: Exploration of science

Relevant parts of the programme of study

Children will be encouraged to develop their investigative skills and understanding of science in the context of:

Explorations and investigations largely of the 'Do . . .', 'Describe which
. . .', and 'Find a Way to . . .' type, involving problems with obvious key
variables which can be solved using a qualitative approach and which
are set within the everyday experience of the children.

(DES 1991d)

These activities will involve children in:

- planning;
- carrying out;
- interpreting;
- drawing inferences;
- communicating.

Profile component 2: Knowledge and understanding of science

A large number of parts of the programme of study will be relevant. In
particular the following related attainment targets:

AT2   Children will have opportunities to find out about a variety of
      animal and plant life.
AT3   Children will be finding out about themselves, developing ideas
      about how they grow, feed, move and use their senses. They will
      be introduced to ideas about how to keep healthy.
AT6   Children will find similarities and differences in a variety of every-
      day materials, including cooking ingredients. They will work with
      and change some of these materials by simple processes such as
      dissolving, heating.
AT13 Children will consider the foods they eat and why they eat them.
      They will talk or communicate by other means about what they eat
      and why and when they eat. They will explore the effect of heating
      substances in order to come to an understanding of the role of
      heating and cooling in bringing about change.

Attainment targets, statements of attainment

The attainment targets and statements of attainment for science indicated in
Figures 4.2 and 4.3 can be covered throughout the topic.

At the outset, a plan of possible ways of developing starting points was
outlined. The following text details one possible plan.

For lunch today

What did we eat?

The starting point is clearly the content of the children's lunches on the
particular day on which the investigation starts. Each child is asked to

AT	Level 1	Level 2	Level 3
1	✓	✓	✓
2	✓	✓	✓
3	✓	✓	
4	✓		
5	✓	✓	
6	✓	✓	
9		✓	
11		✓	
13	✓	✓	✓
15	✓		
16		✓	

Figure 4.2 For lunch today: summary of attainment targets covered

make a list of and draw what he or she had eaten. Further investigation and discussion should reveal a more detailed analysis of the food that has been eaten, that is, what was it made of, what main ingredients were necessary, what was actually eaten? For example, cabbage was the leaves of a plant that grows in the ground, fish fingers had been frozen, lamb is meat which comes from a particular farm animal, etc.

Probably the school cook/mum or dad can be interviewed as a method of investigation. Children should have suggestions about how to find out things they don't know; for example, ask the person who made the lunch or bought the food. Then note what was left over – in preparation and on the plate – food scraps, packaging, waste. What happens to this? Can it be used again? – (compost . . . natural decay of materials . . . disposal of waste from the school kitchen and from home).

Where did it come from?

Children are to investigate (using books, charts, pictures) where the food actually came from. For example, potatoes (from a plant that grows in the ground), lamb (from an animal that lived on a farm), bread for sandwiches (from wheat that grew in a field).

Topic Starting Point   Attainment Targets Relevant for 5–7 years

Topic Starting Point	Levels	1	2	3	4	5	6	7	8	9	10	11	12	13	14	15	16
Question 1	1			✓		✓											
What did we eat?	2					✓											
	3																
Question 2	1																
Where did it come from?	2		✓														
	3		✓														
Question 3	1						✓										
How had the food changed?	2						✓					✓					
	3													✓			
Question 4	1													✓			
How much did we eat?	2		✓	✓			✓							✓			✓
	3																
Question 5	1		✓											✓	✓		
Why did we eat it?	2		✓											✓			
	3		✓											✓			
Question 6	1		✓			✓								✓			
Who needs food?	2		✓														
	3		✓			✓											

Figure 4.3 Location of science attainment targets and statements of attainment within topic if the outset plan detailed in the text is followed

Children should discover that all of their food came from either animals (including fish) or plants, and learn that these are the two basic sources of food for all living things. Most people eat both plant and animals, although some prefer not to eat animals.

Ideas about farming could be introduced. A farmer's job is to rear animals and grow plants for living things to eat. All of these things ultimately depend on the soil. Without the soil there would be no plants. Without plants there would be no animal or human life.

How had the food changed?

That is, how is the food on our plate different in appearance, colour, texture, etc., from its original state as animal or plant? The following ideas should emerge:

- Food can be frozen, packaged, preserved, powdered, etc.
- What are additives? Where does colour come from – natural or otherwise?
- How does cooking change food? (colour, texture, flavour, solid/liquid states). For example, a chip bears no resemblance to a potato tuber, neither does a crisp. The process of changing a potato into a chip or crisp could be investigated.
- What is cooking? Heating substances to change them into a form in which we wish to eat them.
- What supplies the heat? Electricity (discuss sources, safety and dangers of using).
- Does food *have* to be cooked? What is good to eat raw? What was not cooked in your lunch? Would you like to eat a diet of raw food?

How much did we eat?

Class consumption can be worked out. For example, this class ate x potatoes, x fish fingers etc. Once again, the cook can be interviewed. How much food is needed to supply the whole school? Other questions could be:

- How much food do we need? This depends on why we need food.
- Do some people eat more food than they need? Do some people eat less food than they need? This can lead into ideas and discussion about diets.
- How much do you weigh? How much should you weigh? Illnesses associated with too much and too little food.
- What is healthy eating? It important to eat the right kinds of food. Are there 'good' foods and 'bad' foods? Notion of a balanced diet – includes a variety of foods. Could you live on chips?
- Does the world have enough food? Third world situation. Why? Introduce ideas about weather and drought. Rain and good soil are necessary to grow good food.

- Space food – if you left the earth, would you still need food? What food do astronauts eat? What would it look like?

Why did we eat it?

Children will no doubt make suggestions, including 'Because it looked or smelled good' (what is important about the appearance and smell of food? Colour? Presentation? Discuss strong flavours, spices, seasonings. How does cooking affect taste?), 'because I was hungry', 'our bodies tell us when we need food', 'because our bodies need food'.

The key concept is that food is for energy. Without food we would not be able to run, jump, skip, move about. Ultimately we would die. We need food for: energy, nutrients (all the things our bodies need to work properly and repair themselves); and growth and repair to our bodies.

Energy and digestion can be investigated, including the roles of teeth and stomach, for example.

All of these ideas can be investigated, with plenty of scope for practical work.

Who needs food?

- Do all living things need food?
- How do animal diets differ from human diets? Some animals are carnivores, some are herbivores.
- Do animals cook their food?
- What are food chains? The balance of nature. Extinction of species may result if key members of a food chain are missing.
- Do we all like to eat the same things?
- Are there kinds of food we do not eat? Things not good to eat. Bacteria on food, salmonella in eggs, etc.
- What is vegetarianism? Plan your ideal meal.

Implementation

From this planned framework for possible development, the topic progressed in such a way that a large amount of practical investigation and discovery took place. Inevitably, not all of the framework suggestions were taken up and to a large extent the children themselves were the driving force behind progress and content. Results of the initial investigation showed that on the day in question, thirteen children in the class had eaten lamb, seven had eaten fish fingers and eight had brought sandwiches from home. These facts were recorded in writing and in the form of graphical representation. The next major phase of work derived from a visit to the school kitchen and an interview with the cook. This

proved to be a fascinating experience for the children and highly illuminating in terms of revealing children's pre-existing ideas about food
and cookery. In particular, they were overwhelmed with the sheer size of
cooking utensils, pots and pans. 'I had a photograph took holding a pan',
the pan is rather wider than the child in question! This led to lengthy
discussions about the size and scale of the operation and the differences
between the content of home kitchens and the school kitchen. 'Shopping'
for school lunch was a source of great interest with many of the children
in agreement that the cook went off to Sainsbury's with shopping bags
and 'all the cooks went to help carry it'! The whole world of delivery
lorries and shopping in bulk was open for discussion and investigation.
The school cook was wonderfully helpful and provided opportunities for
studying the kitchen equipment, observing the preparation and actual
cooking of food and discussing menus, planning, ordering, delivery,
choice of food and kitchen hygiene.

The class teacher skilfully linked this visit and the myriad of opportunities it provided to the children's knowledge and understanding of
their kitchens at home, when their own families shopped, where the food
originated, and from there into an in-depth investigation of fruits and
vegetables. Practical work at this stage involved close observation and
recording of the size, colour and texture of a variety of fruits and vegetables, putting them into sets, cutting them up, discussions about raw and
cooked food, study of seeds, sorting seeds by size, designing a seed
packet, germinating seeds and monitoring growth bearing in mind conditions for germination. A lot of investigatory and experimental work
took place, guided by the children themselves and their suggestions for
practical work. Seeds were grown under differing conditions and the
results recorded pictorially. The children became personally involved
with their 'own' group's dish of seeds, closely monitoring its progress day
by day. 'Let's visit dish 3 in the fridge' was a common cry! Indeed, the
dishes took on personalities of their own.

One of the most successful aspects of the topic involved making a
'kitchen' in the classroom. This activity was entirely child centred, with the
kitchen contents readily appearing from home. Beakers, whisks, bowls, jugs,
pots, pans and cutlery were loaned and domestic role play took on a whole
new meaning as the children 'beat up cakes like mother does'. This is a
wonderful example of how the resources provided were guiding and giving
structure to the children's activities, and where experiences brought from
home were incorporated into new learning situations.

In the contextual surroundings of the kitchen, various cookery
activities were undertaken, for example, making gingerbread, jelly and
pastry. Jelly making was inevitably a popular activity, through which the
children had practical first-hand experiences of the way in which solid
and liquid states can change, the effects of heating and cooling, change of

texture and the properties of change when ingredients are mixed. Similarly, the pastry making activities involved observations, discoveries and predictions relating to texture and change of texture, mixing solids and liquids, the mixing of ingredients, and the effect of heat on materials. Safety and sources of energy were other important aspects of science incorporated into the cookery lessons. Within the pastry making activity a detailed discussion of the appropriateness of different sieves was an excellent way of developing the concept of fair-testing. Sieves of different sizes were tested to see which was the most effective for sieving different materials, for example, sugar and flour. Indeed, selection of appropriate materials for a task was a key aspect of all kitchen and cookery activities. Without doubt, a substantial amount of the 'subject matter' of science was introduced and developed through the thematic approach adopted.

In addition to the kitchen, a classroom shop was also established, this deriving from investigations into where their own food supplies at home came from. The shop was regularly 'open' providing scope for much mathematical work as the following conversation demonstrates:

Jane: It's my turn to be the shopkeeper now.
Byron: All right.
Brenda: Go behind the counter then.
Nicola: Tell us when you are ready.
Jane: Shop's open now.
Byron: Where's the baskets?
Jane: There aren't none. You'll have to pretend.
Brenda: I'm going to have one of these.
Jane: A packet of cornflakes.
Brenda: How much is that?
Jane: Eighty pence, please.
Brenda: I've only got a pound. Have you got any change?
Jane: I think so.
Byron: Twenty pence change.
Jane: I know! Twenty pence change, madam.
Brenda: Thank you.
Jane: Who's next? Hurry up, somebody.
Nicola: I'm still deciding.
Byron: You shouldn't rush your customers.
Nicola: They don't rush in our corner shop.
Jane: Come on.
Byron: All right. I want a bottle of pop and a packet of crisps.
Jane: Please.
Byron: Please.
Jane: What flavour crisps do you want?
Byron: I'll have cheese and onion, I think. They're my favourites.

Jane:	Sorry, sir, we don't have that flavour. We've got plain, or salt and vinegar or crispy bacon.
Byron:	Better make it salt and vinegar. And some pop.
Jane:	Please.
Byron:	What?
Jane:	Never mind. What sort of pop do you like?
Byron:	What have you got?
Jane:	Lemonade and orange juice and cola.
Byron:	I'll have cola.
Jane:	Do you want a can or a bottle?
Byron:	A bottle.
Jane:	Please!
Byron:	A bottle, please. How much? Please.
Jane:	Let's see. The crisps are ten pence a packet, and the cola is forty-nine pence. That's fifty-nine pence altogether.
Byron:	Please.
Jane:	Fifty-nine pence, please.
Byron:	I've got a fifty and a ten so I need 1p. change . . .
Jane: Byron:	PLEASE!

One of the most interesting outcomes of this practical work was that the children themselves suggested that the shop ought to be linked to the kitchen – with goods transferring from one to the other – hence the two were seen to be in close association with each other.

The nature of the organisation of the topic as a whole reflected the teacher's commitment to a child-centred approach and cooperative group work. A number of class-based starting points were discussed, then followed up by individuals or in groups. Recording of learning and activities undertaken by the children was done in a variety of ways, ranging from the traditional (block graphs and writing an account of what had been done) to the innovative (designing a seed packet with instructions for would-be sowers, and writing recipe cards). Every child entered work in an individual topic workbook and contributed to class displays. Other recording was in the form of photographs, audio tape and video tape. The topic was developed and recorded in a wholly integrated, cross-curricular manner. A great deal of mathematics and language work underpinned and reinforced the scientific content and creative and aesthetic development was evident throughout, for example, art work, drama and music ('The Gingerbread Man').

An analysis of the overall approach to development reveals a very successful mixing of the three starting points articulated earlier in this chapter, namely the children's own experiences, a topic, and the subject matter of science.

In conclusion, therefore, it is evident that the overall approach to organisation of learning in this case study was a topic deriving from the children's daily routine. This was the unifying element, enabling aspects of learning to be pursued in an integrated way. As work progressed, a wide range of skills, concepts, knowledge, understanding and attitudes were introduced and developed across a range of areas of learning.

This case study has shown how a topic can successfully be used as a basis for development of a core area and act as a unifying element in the integration of children's work. Within this structure it is totally appropriate to introduce the subject matter of science for its own sake from time to time. A good example of this in the case study was the pastry making session. The teacher used cookery as an opportunity to develop the concept of fair-testing and organised the means for investigations so that the children were ably to fairly test various sieves and arrive at conclusions relating to their suitability for dealing with different materials. This is one of a number of occasions when the subject matter of science was highlighted and 'taught' for its own sake.

It must also be emphasised that underpinning successful topic work such as this is the great wealth of personal experience that the children themselves bring to a learning environment. In the case study, the teacher was not only aware of this, but skilfully capitalised upon it and organised and developed it into meaningful learning situations. A good example of how this was to be done is the way in which the topic was encouraged to get off the ground in the first instance. Instead of going 'blindly' into the school kitchen, the children were encouraged to think about the organisation and contents of their own kitchens at home, to talk about their experiences and to bring objects to school that would be useful in setting up the classroom kitchen. Immediately this made for an excellent contrast when children saw the size and scale of the school kitchen and the event was inevitably far more meaningful than it might otherwise have been. The children had a context from their own world in which to encounter and develop new ideas and experiences.

SUMMARY

As a whole, this chapter has attempted to demonstrate how the National Curriculum for science may be used as a framework for Key Stage 1 and not a straitjacket. Well-planned topic work can have a fundamental place within this framework. Documentation provides us with a prescribed and minimum entitlement for each child, yet there is adequate scope for spontaneous work, meaningful links with other areas of learning, and ample opportunity for imaginative practical activities.

The process, however, should not be left to chance. In order to ensure that each infant child gets a broad, balanced and successful science education, every school will need regularly to evaluate its science policy. This need not be a syllabus, rather a statement reflecting the strengths and needs of all children and approaches to teaching and learning so that the school can plan a coordinated and balanced science programme. The staff as a whole need to work as a team, doing rather more than including 'some science' in a theme or topic. Coordinated planning is needed, ensuring that programmes of study are adequately delivered in ways that are appropriate to the school, its children and their processes of learning. In many schools this is done through the continuation of long-established approaches, such as working through themes and topics. Such practice can be ideal as long as it incorporates a coordinated and whole school approach to the range and balance of themes which are studied, and overall progression within science education. It should also incorporate the development of children's natural experiences which are brought to the classroom and a respect for the integrity and subject matter of science. If this is achieved, then its implementation will indeed go a very long way towards forming the building blocks of first-class early years science education.

Chapter 5

Mathematics and topic work

INTRODUCTION

There seems little need to argue that the distinctive nature of mathematics should be preserved in the infant curriculum. In respect of other subjects the need to consider this emphasis has been suggested. In the case of mathematics, this subject, from the days of the old elementary schools up to the present day, has been seen and taught very much as a separate subject. True, we have moved from arithmetic in the elementary schools through what were sometimes rather perfunctory nods at the whole of mathematics before the introduction of the National Curriculum, to a quite broad definition of what should be taught to children at Key Stage 1. It may be the case that mathematics, while preserving its place in its own right in the curriculum, also needs more of a shift than is common into topic work. Mathematics can both support topics and be a topic focus in itself. A topic focused on mathematics can enable children to explore certain areas of the subject to some depth. This benefit of topic work is one which has been stressed throughout this book. It is important that children use and apply mathematics, not only because use enhances understanding but also to enable them to make connections between different parts of mathematics and to see patterns. For example the principles of measurement in length, weight, volume, capacity and area are similar. At some point children need to understand this, and a topic bringing these elements together might be beneficial.

Mathematics at Key Stage 1 (DES 1991a) has five attainment targets. The description or definition of the mathematics to be covered in each of these are as follows:

Attainment Target 1: Using and applying mathematics.
Pupils should choose and make use of knowledge, skills and understanding outlined in the programmes of study in practical tasks, in real life problems and to investigate within mathematics itself. Pupils would be expected to use with confidence the appropriate mathematical content

specified in the programme of study relating to other attainment targets.

Attainment Target 2: Number.
Pupils should use and understand number including estimation and approximation, interpreting results and checking for reasonableness.

Attainment Target 3: Algebra.
Pupils should recognise and use symbolic representation to express patterns and relationships.

Attainment Target 4: Shape and space.
Pupils should recognise and use the properties of two and three dimensional shapes and use measurement, location and transformation in the study of space.

Attainment Target 5: (Handling Data, Logic and Probability)
Pupils should collect, process and interpret data and should understand, estimate and use possibilities.

(DES 1991a)

Each attainment target is weighted equally for assessment. The definitions for each attainment target and this equal weighting suggest that the NCC and the DFE have in mind the sort of teaching of mathematics which has been recommended to teachers over a long period of time by Her Majesty's Inspectorate and mathematics educationists. These definitions of the five areas of mathematics specified suggest a number of principles:

1 Children need to use and apply mathematics. Knowing how to do number work is not sufficient; children need to see that their answers make sense.
2 Measurement, that other aspect of quantity, is incorporated where it will be used: in attainment targets 2 and 4. (Remembering that measurement is different from, say, counting discrete items like conkers but applies to continuous quantities like the length of a snail trail or how much this jug holds. What is counted is not the train nor the capacity but the units we use to measure with.)
3 Algebra, which depends on a firm foundation of arithmetic, is about seeing patterns and making connections.
4 Pictorial representation or data handling is included with probability and logic so that the connections between these items can be made.
5 Shape and space is also related to measures.

In short, teachers are being reminded of not only the different areas of mathematics but of their inter-connectedness and how each supports and illuminates the others. At Key Stage 1 young children are to be introduced to mathematics in all these aspects.

Schools and teachers are posed questions about how to implement a curriculum to meet this demand. How far should mathematics be taught as a separate subject? Is there a place for mathematics to be taught separately for its own intrinsic interest? What is the role of mathematics schemes? How far should mathematics be taught with other subjects and in topics? These are the questions this chapter will attempt to address.

It will be argued that topic work, sensibly managed, may be an essential part of the mathematics curriculum in the classroom. It can provide necessary vehicles for the use and application of mathematics. It can also deepen understanding where suitable mathematical concepts are selected as a topic focus. *Mathematics 5–11: A Handbook of Suggestions* (DES 1979) noted that thematic work is suitable for introducing some mathematics providing the teacher has sufficient knowledge of the subject to find the potential within the topic. Such opportunities, it added, can be missed. However they concluded:

> The thematic approach is unlikely to motivate all the mathematics which most children need to cover within the age range 5–11 years: it is necessary to provide adequate time for mathematics, to cover a scheme of work systematically and to include regular revision of those skills which have been identified as necessary for further progress.
>
> (HMI 1979 ibid.)

This was written in 1979. More than a decade later, a similar view is being taken, but offering ways in which teachers might seize opportunities to use topic work productively. This chapter will not be unrealistic about teaching mathematics. Topic work and separate work on mathematics including the use of mathematics schemes (which are widely used and possess many advantages) can both form part of the variety of situations that we suggest are necessary to learning. Both may be necessary if the mathematics curriculum is to be broad and balanced and the aims of mathematics education in the early years are to be met.

In this chapter we suggest ways in which mathematics can be used to support topics. Two mathematically focused topics will also be outlined. To set the scene, however, the context in which children learn mathematics in school will be discussed, starting with aims for teaching.

THE AIMS OF MATHEMATICS EDUCATION

The aim of mathematics education in the early years at school might be broadly defined as 'to establish the foundations of mathematical thinking'. To this end children do need to learn those basic skills which require practice and procedural knowledge. They need to know how to count, how to add, subtract, multiply and divide. Note the words 'how to'.

Thinking with and about mathematics needs to go beyond 'how to' to why. Why does this work? Can it be generalised to other situations? This may not occur if all the knowledge that children have is procedural. Learning a procedure is familiar to all of us who remember the instruction 'invert and multiply' when faced with the division of fractions. This is a useful and powerful algorithm, as are those for subtraction using either the equal addition or the regrouping (decomposing) methods. What many of us did not know as we were taught, was why some procedures and algorithms worked. Knowing how to do something may have been a poor substitute for understanding it and being able to generalise our knowledge. This principle applies equally to young children. When children ask 'is this an add or a take away?' it may be a danger signal that they are applying procedures and may not be in a position to transfer and generalise what is known to other situations.

It is not necessarily the case that being taught how to do something but not why, will prevent children from understanding the mathematics, but it is certainly a strong possibility. An example is a child coping admirably in a year 3 class with the addition, including carrying, of four digit numbers. However, when she was asked what her answer (5374) was, she said very indignantly 'I don't know' (implied – why should I?). If she were unable to say that her total was five thousand, three hundred and seventy four one would suspect that her grasp of place value was shaky. Nevertheless, she could get the right answers. Similarly, the over-generalisation of a rule or procedure might cause a child to take both of the smaller digits from the larger in a sum like 43 subtract 28.

Children, it is suggested, may be successful at using procedures yet unable to generalise or use their knowledge. A major finding of the Cockroft Report (Cockroft 1982) was that levels of attainment in mathematics were better than the Committee of Inquiry had been led to expect. Many children had basic skills in mathematics and these were well covered in schools. What children could not do was to use this knowledge in other situations or to solve real life problems. They could not generalise or transfer their knowledge. It is not sufficient, to illustrate this at a narrow and basic level, to be able to add or subtract or multiply or divide in your workbook if you cannot transfer these skills into shopping (in a real shop with real money). Will you be able to generalise and understand that a triangle is any two-dimensional shape bounded by three straight lines if you are always presented with equilateral triangles? Will you know that a pentagon can include a concave angle if you only see regular pentagons and are not told that these are regular?

Many educationists (Cockroft, 1982, Desforges and Cockburn 1987, Skemp 1989) criticise mathematics education which focuses too much on procedural knowledge and inhibits the ability to understand and generalise. This does not mean that practising basic skills, for example, is wrong. Practice, to enable children to use skills quickly and automatically, is essential (Bennett *et al.* 1984). Indeed, it has been found that practice of lower order skills can lead to the development of higher order skills. For example, children practising counting all when adding have invented counting on (from the first group of numbers) (Gelman and Gallistell 1978). Similarly, two children who did not understand the basis of place value were found to do so after three weeks of working through exercises on place value and with no other teaching (Desforges and Cockburn 1987). Nevertheless, it is sensible to suppose that it is often the case that children cannot easily transfer what they can do from one situation to another, which for them is very different. They may be familiar, say, with subtraction defined as 'take away' and be thrown by 'difference'. These two elements of subtraction *are* different but employ the same minus symbol. Adults take this for granted. Children often do not. If the mathematics they are asked to do is limited to a narrow and linear progression by the use of workbooks or sheets, they may fail to make the connection between, in this case, the complex uses of one symbol. More broadly, unless they meet mathematics in a range of different situations and the connections between the mathematics met in these situations is drawn to their attention, they may lose their early enthusiasm and understanding of what they are about. They may cease to think any further than whether the sum has the right answer. It is suggested, therefore, that teachers need to consider whether they can provide a variety of situations for learning mathematics and in particular about how they use their mathematics scheme.

MATHEMATICS SCHEMES

We define mathematics schemes as either those schemes which are commercially available or those compiled by teachers, often using a variety of commercial schemes as a source for ideas. In either event the schemes of work which we consider might be inadequate are those in which workbooks, worksheets or work-cards predominate or are the only materials used. There is no doubt that most schools use a scheme of this sort to some extent. Such schemes provide a wealth of attractive material a busy teacher could not possibly prepare. Modern commercial schemes are based on the National Curriculum and the best schemes provide excellent handbooks which suggest practical work and items for discussion and use across the curriculum. In addition to these advantages, many teachers, like many of the general public, feel insecure about mathematics and feel that the commercial schemes, written by experts, provide structure and security.

However, we are suggesting that schemes can be a good servant but a bad master. Obviously children's progress in mathematics, to meet the aims we have outlined above, will depend on how a scheme is used. A scheme, by its nature, must be designed as if every child who encounters it learns in the same order, needs to do every page, and that those pages which are included are sufficient for every child. If the scheme, only the scheme and all of the scheme is used, there is little possibility of children enjoying mathematics in the different situations which we have suggested are essential. Children may be thought to be progressing at their own pace. In practice, some of them may not be progressing at all. Teaching may be restricted to fielding problems when children get stuck. It is rather difficult to explain and get to the root of the problems in this situation and the temptation is to show the child the correct procedure again (Bennett *et al.* 1984). If the work is too hard, much time may be wasted in queues. If it is too easy, children are unlikely to say so.

A less obvious disadvantage of using a scheme is the 'racetrack' mentality which may develop (Desforges and Cockburn 1987). Children can become very hooked on progress, motivated by ticks, completed pages and having the next book. In fact, it may become quite difficult to drag them away from what they see as the real mathematics work in the classroom to engage in a mathematical game or investigation. Besides, away from the printed page, they may be asked to do something which makes their brains 'hurt' a little and children are no keener on doing that than other people. The printed page also has problems related to practical work. If measurement is taken as an example, its comparative nature cannot really be established from drawings or pictures. Is a tree taller than a house? It depends. Is the dog in this picture heavier than the elephant in this picture? The printed page does not permit children to do real measurement, which is a pity because the classroom is full of things which can be handled and compared to begin the process of understanding the uses of measuring, the skills to be deployed and the comparisons needed.

Schemes can be and often are used positively. Of course, handbooks and teachers' guides need to be studied critically. To ensure that children get appropriate help they might be grouped roughly by attainment so that sections of the scheme can be taught before they are attempted. Teachers also need to know schemes well. Not all children will need to do all the pages but others will need extra practice. If certain pages invariably disconcert some children it is likely that there is something wrong with the pages not the children. Sometimes these pages are simply in the wrong order in respect of what children know. It has to be said that occasionally the mathematics in some schemes is dubious and teachers should not always assume that the authors know best.

It is important to try to make time for observation. It is very difficult to assess what children can actually do unless the teacher can observe them working in their scheme books from time to time. Children copy, look back at previous answers and remember what the teacher said the answer was (Desforges and Cockburn 1987). Given a page of correct sums a teacher cannot tell afterwards what strategies were used. All answers may be correct but if the page were about addition one child might have counted all, one counted on from one of the numbers, one used his or her fingers, one known the answer instantly and one could not do them at all but was helped by the teacher. If the intention of the page was that children should use carrying in addition, that is that the sums were of the type 17 + 6 written vertically, none of the children (except the one who requested help), would have used the correct strategy.

Many teachers use schemes solely for practice, for revision or for a check on attainment. When children are confident about the mathematics they do in this way, they can go quickly through the pages, get a sense of achievement and the teacher is freed for other work.

Careful selection of a scheme is necessary although cost is an ever present constraint. It is well worth taking the time, however, to use teachers' centres, training institutions and visits to other schools to see schemes in action before selecting one to buy. In spite of all this, however, we have to say that a scheme may well be necessary, especially in saving the teacher's time and sanity, but it cannot on its own be sufficient if the aims we have outlined for mathematics education are to be attempted.

To summarise, the mathematics curriculum may well include a scheme. In planning, the school and individual teachers will take the scheme into account together with other systematic coverage of the curriculum which might be needed over and above the mathematics arising in their topics. This coverage would include games, practical applications of mathematics, problem solving and investigations. Some of these activities might arise in topic work but this should not be at the cost of making strained or tenuous connections with the major focus. Putting sums into outline drawings of candles at Christmas, where the topic is mainly scientific and candle flames are being observed and investigated adds nothing to either the mathematics or the science. (Although it may be fun and there is nothing against that.) However, there are plenty of sensible links to be made between mathematics and the rest of the curriculum. Some examples will be given in the next section.

MATHEMATICS ACROSS THE CURRICULUM

Mathematics is obviously necessary to the development of learning in many other areas of the curriculum. Where such learning is to be topic based, planning a topic should start with learning specific to the major subject or subjects to be covered. Planning can then be extended to other necessary support including mathematics. In some cases mathematics has to be involved, in others it will be a useful adjunct. It would be necessary to use mathematics to support science if measurement were required, for example, of temperature or rainfall or the distance objects would travel under different conditions. The various forms in which data can be represented is not only part of the mathematics curriculum but also essential to display and ease of reference in science and in other subjects. The reference to a useful adjunct is where mathematics might not be essential but would be appropriate and included in order to promote the coverage of the mathematics curriculum. It might not be necessary to use a preference graph, for example, in a topic on food. If practice of this form were needed by the class it would, however, form a useful comparison with an essential graph about nutritional value, add a dimension, and provide practice. However, the mathematics to be used across the curriculum needs to be considered carefully for several reasons.

Some mathematics which must be used to support other subjects may not be at the right level. That is, in a topic on minibeasts in year 2 it would be necessary to count the minibeasts' legs (if they had any). Although this would be necessary to classification it would not be likely to benefit more than a few year 2 children mathematically. So far as development in mathematics is concerned, the levels of attainment in the class need to be considered. In the mini-beasts example, counting legs would be necessary but could not be stated to be a mathematical objective for all children. However this example also demonstrates that, in a topic, children at various levels of attainment can contribute and participate at their own level. A few year 2 children might be challenged by simple counting or need practice. The majority might be challenged by measurement of the animals or their tracks in centimetres.

When looking for mathematical concepts at appropriate levels of attainment the question of those which would be useful to the topic but are just too difficult for anyone in the class also have to be thought through. Numbers can get very large very quickly, for example, if area is being measured. Measurement of irregular items such as leaves also brings in those awkward bits which are fractions. A task can be simplified. Leaves can be placed on top of each other for comparison of area and large squared paper solves some of the problems of the fractions. Nevertheless, the mathematics should not be distorted. When dealing with fractions children should not be encouraged to call a 'bit over' a half if this is wildly inaccurate. Children should be challenged to use their existing mathematics but within sensible limits. Having said that, it can be stressed that within reason, children can often go further than might be predicted when they are presented with a problem or task which it seems necessary to deal with. Calculators enable children to use larger numbers without too much tedious working out or possibility of error once the principles of the calculation have been grasped.

Mathematics supporting or being used as a tool in topics will meet much of attainment target 1 – using and applying mathematics. Again care must be taken when considering levels. The first item in attainment targets 1, 2 and 3 exemplify the wide difference between these levels:

Level 1 – using mathematics for a practical task . . . .
Level 2 – selecting the materials and the mathematics for a practical task . . . .
Level 3 – selecting the materials and the mathematics to use for a practical task using alternative approaches to overcome difficulties.

(DES 1991a)

The non-statutory examples matching these attainment targets (DES 1991a), (remembering that these are the *sorts* of activities children should be able to do), underline this progression. It may be all too easy to assume that the attainment target is being met if any practical application is made but there is a huge difference between being *given* materials to do a task and *selecting* the materials. Perhaps it can be stressed again that a challenge is often met if the situation makes sense to children and demands that they think about it. Learning even in mathematics is not entirely hierarchical. Children will always surprise us by their thinking and strategies, and should never be underestimated.

Naturally, number will figure prominently in topics. However, measures and data handling (which will include number where appropriate) may merit further discussion. The measurement of length, weight, volume, capacity area and time will often be needed across the curriculum. Frequently this will be the sort of measurement which is valuable precisely because the results will be unpredictable (unlike measuring a line in a mathematics work-book). Measurement is never precise or exact but depends on the accuracy (which can be extended indefinitely) of the measuring device used. This important principle in measurement is hard to get over to children because they like a right answer. Measuring in a situation where the result is unlikely to be 'exact' draws attention to the idea of 'betweeness' and the approximate nature of all measurement. Measurement used for a real purpose (often but not exclusively in science) will normally have this aspect. For example, one of the minibeasts mentioned above might be more than $8 1/2$ but less than 9 cm long. Being as accurate as possible (i.e. using and applying the skills of measurement) will frequently arise, for example, in technology. It is not hard to see that opportunities for using skills, practice, enrichment and new learning in measurement are legion in topics.

It is worth considering precisely how measurement or any other mathematical skill or knowledge is to be included in topic work. If the skill or concept is new it might be sensible to teach it as a separate activity before using it. An example will illustrate this point. If children are going to be asked to weigh themselves using bathroom-type scales, the figure in kilograms on the dial will be very abstract. Work leading up to the use of the scales with a spring balance and homemade elastic weighing devices, and then comparison with the scales would make an understanding of how bathroom scales work clearer and also introduce ideas about forces. If, on the other hand, children already had skills to be utilised in a topic, it might be useful to revise these skills before using them. Children might need to be reminded *how* to use handspans or a rule or a metre stick properly before measuring, and that, in measurement, an appropriate unit should be selected (for example, not to use teaspoons to fill a bucket).

Estimation in measurement also makes sense in topic work because reasons for estimation can be identified. About how many metre sticks will we need to measure our planned wild garden? This sort of practice is essential to estimation. You cannot estimate unless you have used a particular measuring unit frequently. This is the difference between an estimate, which is based on experience, and a guess which is random.

The measurement of money is rather different from any other sort of measurement because the units, normally coins at this level, have no logical relationship to each other in size or colour. On the whole, shops and shopping which use money can be topics in themselves, often linked to industrial and commercial understanding with visits to shops, school sales and visits to small businesses.

Reference to chapter 6 indicates the relationship between measurement and graphicacy. Coordinates may also be used in mathematics in addition or multiplication squares or in geography through map making. Which comes first is immaterial. That the principal is the same is the important point. As mentioned earlier, opportunities for data handling can be found in many topics. Simple databases on a computer can be used in the early years classroom in many subject areas. For example, such a database might be used in history and geography. An examination of the forms in which data can be represented set out in the National Curriculum (DES 1991a) shows a rich variety of methods.

At or approaching level 1, topics centred on the children themselves are common and appropriate. Often, the most useful representations of data allied to these topics are sets (rather than graphs) which can be interpreted readily if the numbers are kept small. Examples are children on this table who have blue eyes and those who have brown eyes, or those who stay to dinner and those who do not stay to dinner. In other topics at this level, sets using actual objects can be used: these float, these sink or these were attracted by a magnet and those were not. Such displays are arresting and avoid, in respect of floating and sinking, a lot of soggy, inaccurate drawing. Simple intersecting sets, Venn diagrams and relationships specified by arrows are the next steps. Another represen- tation using sets is the birthday train, which has a cut out of each child in the carriage labelled with the appropriate month.

First graphs are block graphs where the data are counted, not read off, so a vertical axis is not necessary. Strip graphs record actual measurement, using a strip of paper cut to show actual height or the distance round children's heads. Often strips need to be ordered, say tallest to shortest, so the data are clear. Bar charts, where the data must be read off and cannot be counted, come at level 3. The National Curriculum identifies progression in respect of what children can probably cope with. It is also important to consider the best methods of displaying and representing the data. These are not necessarily the same thing. Of course, the method selected should not be one which the children cannot yet understand, like a bar chart in reception. The best way to represent data may well be one which they know well. The progression in mathematics for children in this instance is the ability to decide the best method or methods to use, which will not necessarily be the most advanced in their repertoire. Considering which is most appropriate might avoid the ubiquitous presence of the block graph. Use of data handling in a topic demands the indication of relationships which do or do not exist, the clarity of the information presented and the arresting nature of the display, which can go beyond colouring in squares.

A profitable addition to topics focused on other subjects are topics focused on mathematics itself. Two such topics will be outlined in the final section.

TWO TOPICS FOCUSED ON MATHEMATICS

Neither of these topics have been taught in exactly the form that follows. Both have had to be updated to meet current attainment targets in mathematics. Some revisions and additions have been made with the intention of improvement in the light of hindsight and reflection. However, all the content has been taught in one form or other and has been found to work in classrooms. Material has been drawn from personal experience and from the work of PGCE students whose contributions are acknowledged. The assessment procedures suggested for the first topic have been abridged and made manageable to teachers from the Durham project on children's knowledge of mathematics when they enter school (Aubrey and Pettitt in progress).

A mathematics topic for the reception class – counting

Introduction

For various reasons a great many children enter reception classes when they are 4 years old. Some are barely 4. The topic outlined here is designed for these children to take place soon after they enter school. It would also be appropriate for older children in a nursery. It is important to see the curriculum from 3 to 8 (and beyond) as continuous and coherent. Having said that, children of 4 are similar to older children in that they will have very different experiences and attainments. In addition, teachers, in spite of liaison with nurseries and parents, may have less information to go on as they attempt to match the curriculum to the children. In other classes the school will have very detailed records which are passed up with the children. What we know with some certainty is that many children of 4 come to school knowing a good deal about mathematics, especially about number. This was discussed in some detail in chapter 1. The problem for reception teachers is that they need to find out what this knowledge is and to tailor their curricula to it. The topic we suggest, therefore, is heavily geared to assessment of an unthreatening and tentative nature. Reception class teachers, during the children's early time in school, are in a good position to assess what children know as they settle them into school and set up regimes where, for a large part of the time children will be doing activities with sand, water, paint, constructional toys and all the equipment and organisation of a good nursery class.

Reception class teachers are not bound to begin to implement the National Curriculum until the term in which children become 5. They are, however, working towards level 1 in the National Curriculum before that. Working towards level 1 with these young children needs to focus on oral and practical work, but not in the first instance, recording. This is not to say they should be prevented from trying their hand at writing, for example. However, things they can do already, that is, talking, using their senses and showing by actions what they know, should be encouraged. This should precede trying to write numbers before they can count or recognise them, or before their fine motor control can deal with recording in writing. Starting the mathematics curriculum by writing numbers and drawing sets of 2 and then 3 and then 4 and so on, which is common in mathematics schemes, can hold children back. To be stuck on 2 (notoriously hard to write) is demoralising, especially if children can count, as some can, to 20 or more, and especially if they can deal with the principles of counting which we show below.

We have selected counting for our topic because there is clear evidence that it is fundamental to what follows in number (Young-Loveridge 1987). Common sense indicates that if you cannot count, addition and subtraction within the number that can be counted, are impossible. Counting leads naturally into counting on (one form of addition) and to seeing how many more are needed (one form of subtraction). It is also something that young children love to do. Parents count with children – their toes, their steps – from an early age, and it is often quite hard and indeed unnecessary to stop them counting.

The aims and objectives of the topic

The aim of this topic is to work towards appropriate sections of attainment target 2 level 1 of the National Curriculum in mathematics. This aim relates to only a part of the relevant programme of study which states that children should:

- engage in activities which involve *counting*, reading, writing and ordering numbers to at least 10; and
- *learn that the size of a set is given by the last number in the count.*

The parts in italics are the first steps. Some children may go on to read and order and a few to write numbers.

In order to get at objectives for learning it is necessary to break down exactly what we mean by being able to count. Counting involves:

- *Recitation*: Numbers have names (1, 2, 3, etc.) and children learn how to chant these names. At first this is fairly meaningless to them but is nevertheless an important step.
- *Stable order*: The children learn that there is an agreed stable order for counting which has to be used.
- *One:one principle*: The stable order is mapped onto the one:one principle. That is, in an array of objects each one is counted once and once only. Children have to remember that 'I've counted those and I've still got to count those'. This is what makes drawing objects while counting them so hard. While children are trying to draw they forget about the count.
- *The cardinal principle*: The last object counted gives the size of the set.
- *Order irrelevance*: It does not matter in what order an array is counted, as long as you count once and once only, you will get the same number.

Abstracted from all this is the idea that you can count anything. If you count five elephants or five ants you will still get five.

This breakdown of counting gives us our objectives for most children in reception classes. They require that children count as high as they can, that they count from left to right and right to left, objects in a line, in a pile, in a circle, from the first object in the line or the second and so on. Children should be able to give someone three objects from a pile of ten or eight objects from twelve. In short, they need to do a lot of counting of real objects.

Further objectives for more able children are that they should be able to put numbers in the right order and understand that three comes before four and after two and so on. These children should also begin to recognise written numbers.

As the topic includes stories and rhymes and naturally a good deal of talking English, objectives can be set:

Working towards Attainment Target 1 Level 1
- (a) participate as speakers and listeners in group activities including imaginative play
- (b) listen attentively, and respond to stories and poems
- (c) respond appropriately to simple instructions given by the teacher

Working towards Attainment Target 4 Level 1
- (a) begin to show an understanding of the difference between drawing and writing and between numbers and letters.

(DES 1990a)

Content and learning

Each of the three weeks for which the work is planned will have a similar content but will have at its core a different story involving numbers. (Other stories will be included not related to number but continuing traditional tales, e.g. Red Riding Hood. In a multi-cultural class, traditional stories from children's own culture can be included.)

Week 1

- *Focus story*:   Goldilocks and the Three Bears
- *Other stories*:   Three Billy Goats Gruff; Three Little Pigs (unless there are Muslim children in the class).
- *Rhymes*:   Drawn from teacher's repertoire of number rhymes especially where action is required. Some can be adapted to fit the focus story, e.g. instead of 'one elephant was balancing . . .', use 'One teddy bear was balancing round and round on a piece of string. He was having such enormous fun he asked another teddy bear to come. How many now?' etc.
- *Home corner*:   Each week this is set up to fit the focus story. In week 1 it will be the three bears' house. Teachers will intervene to ensure bowls, chairs, beds. etc. are counted.
- *Games*:   Simple counting games (detailed below).
- *Class activities*: Counting, recorded with beads on a string or something similar, of number of boys and girls here today, number absent, children staying to dinner, having packed lunch or going home. Making sets of children according to colour of socks and other characteristics, and counting them. Voting, for example on how many children are allowed in the three bears' house at once. Other activities: (1) A large number track 1 to 10 under which trays or shoe boxes are positioned. Children are asked to put the appropriate number of objects in each

box. Working in pairs one child checks the other. (2) A large drawing of some fields in which numbers are placed on cards so the numbers can be changed. Children put the right numbers of farm animals or zoo animals in the fields. (3) Number jigsaws, dominoes, etc. as available. (4) Children make numbers from Plasticine and stick the correct numbers of buttons on each number. The writing corner will ask 'Can you write these numbers?' Numbers will be prominently displayed, each having dots which can be counted. (5) The reading area will have the stories being read on display. It will also include simple number books to look at. The learning is drawn from the objectives stated above. Some children will not be able to do those activities related to reading numbers.

Week 2
- *Focus story*:   Snow White and the Seven Dwarfs

Week 3
- *Focus story*:   The Enormous Turnip

Further details

Introduction

The teacher tells the children that she or he has noticed how good they are at counting. They will probably count together to ten to prove it. Teacher continues 'we're going to do lots of work on counting for the class assembly in three weeks' time' (some other purpose might be identified but children like to have a point to their activities). Inviting them to contribute as often as possible, teacher talks about: who counts (shopkeepers), what sorts of things should we count (e.g. why the register) and asks if they know any counting rhymes. They conclude with the focus story.

The assembly

This would be very simple. Possibly children would just act out some of the counting rhymes. Perhaps the children might have numbers on their backs, in groups of one to ten and turn round as they say the number.

Counting games

This refers to very simple board or card games. Most board games consist of a counting track and at this level there is no need to put numbers on the track. Indeed this can be confusing as the numbers would be upside down for some children and would not correspond to the number thrown after the first move. It is useful to have a home not on the track for the counters, so that the children start to count from one, as opposed to starting by putting the counter on one and counting from there. (Zero cannot be included on a number track.) Dice may be thrown, or better, cards with numbers and dots can be drawn, which is quieter. It is important to have some numbers written as numbers, some displayed as dots, preferably in a variety of configurations, and some with both, as counting leads to recognition.

Children storying with or without the teacher

This would be using figures she or he has made from the three focus stories. These can be of stout card or felt, as on a flannel-graph. There are patterns available to knit Snow White and the dwarfs but this is very time consuming unless you can borrow a set. In each case, including the characters from The Enormous Turnip, the characters have numbers on them and the children are encouraged in the stories to count and order the characters. While the children shut their eyes one of the figures, e.g. number six, could be removed from a line (he is hiding). They then have to spot the one that is missing.

Reading

Children like to read songs and rhymes they know by heart. Teachers may like to print the rhymes being used on large cards (like the big books used in many classes) preferably illustrated, which children can share with each other. Children will be found reading these, often in pairs, as they relate the known words to the print. The word 'reading' is used here in the broadest sense.

Assessment

In the first week the children can also be introduced to Not-Very-Clever Ted, a large teddy bear who they can help with his number work. This teddy can be named to start with and children vote on the name. He is then used in the tests shown below. For example, 'Ted can only count to four. How high can you count?' Although a good deal of useful information can be collected to inform future teaching, it is also sensible to seize immediate teaching opportunities in this activity. Often, simply asking children to do something causes them to begin to think and extend what they can already do. This is especially the case if they see helping Ted as fun or a game. It is essential that the assessment is unthreatening and is carried out with familiar material. It is suggested that farm animals, zoo animals, little cars and similar items, are used for counting in preference to counters or cubes.

1 Ask children how high they can count. Prompt one, two, three, if
   necessary.
2 Ask them to count three objects in a line, seven objects in a pile, nine
   objects in a circle.
3 Ask them to give you three objects from a pile of ten and six objects
   from a pile of ten.
4 Ask them to count four objects in a line. If they agree that there are four
   ask them how many there would be if they made the second object on
   the right number one.
5 Show them the numbers one to ten in random order and ask them what
   they are.

Strategies should be noted and, as suggested above, teaching implemented where it seems useful. If children do not have one:one correspondence they may wave their fingers vaguely over the objects. Teacher,
who will be as interested in teaching as testing, may at this point tell the
child we only count each one once; perhaps no one has pointed that out.
Physically moving the objects often helps. In the test of giving three from
ten using animals, it often helps the children to attain the cardinal principle if they are encouraged to first stand all the animals up, then make
the required number lie down. A similar strategy assists with the objects
in a circle. Overall, it is obvious that testing of any sort is always tentative
and provisional and that it may all look very different tomorrow. Nevertheless, combining this topic on number with assessment may lay a solid
foundation for the future work of both teachers and the children.

A topic for year 2 Curves, circles, spheres, cylinders, cones

Introduction

Once more this could be a fairly short topic, perhaps for three weeks, but
it is suggested that it is extended to include non-curved shape. The reason
for this will discussed below. It is likely that many of the class will have
been introduced to two-dimensional and three-dimensional shape. Part
of the purpose of the topic is to provide abler children with an opportunity to broaden and deepen their mathematical understanding of
shape. It is sometimes the case that meeting attainment targets in a fairly
superficial way causes these children to be moved on to the next level.
Often their mathematical thinking can be extended by getting them to
explore, rather more deeply, the concepts they have. In addition, many
children often get rather mixed up about shape and space, particularly the
relationship between two-dimensional and three-dimensional shape, and
a short topic may sort out these problems. These two ideas taken together
illustrate the spiral notion of the curriculum. Learning frequently

involves two steps forward and one step back. To some extent this topic is a step back for consolidation and revision but it also contains what are likely to be new dimensions. The aims of this topic are therefore well spread over levels 1, 2 and 3 of attainment target 4.

Attainment Target 4 level 1
- sort and classify 2 D and 3 D shapes using words such as straight, flat, curved, round etc.

Attainment Target 4 level 2
- recognising squares, rectangles, circles, triangle, hexagons, pentagons, cubes, rectangular boxes (cuboids), cylinders and spheres and describing their properties.

Attainment Target 4 level 3
- sort 2D and 3D shapes giving reasons for their sorting.
- recognising reflective symmetry in a variety of shapes and two and three dimensions.

(DES 1991a)

(It is assumed for the topic, that those children who look at symmetry will have had some prior experience of mirror or reflective symmetry using two-dimensional shape. Level 3 seems a little late for this introduction in our view.)

Once more we need to break these attainment targets down to think about objectives. In the first instance, we are trying to meet these objectives using a particular set of shapes, but later on we will try to find out whether knowledge about these shapes can be used to indicate that similar concepts can be identified about other shapes. This is a further example of the connections children need to make across the mathematics curriculum. It might be best to try to establish our objectives for learning to see what it is about shapes in general, and these shapes in particular, which needs to be taught, and what sorts of problems children may have with earlier knowledge. Five objectives are established here:

1 Children are often confused about the relationship between a two-dimensional and 3-dimensional shape. Often this is because we have had to use solid thin shapes to model two dimensions. The first objective then is to ensure that children get the idea that the *face* of a solid is two-dimensional and that however thin an object is, it is a solid (e.g. a circle cut from paper is a cylinder).

2 In relation to the first objective, children can be asked to explore and learn more about the relationship between two- and three-dimensional shapes by slicing up solids. The second objective then is to find out what happens when this is done and to note (a) the sorts of faces given by horizontal, vertical and sloping cuts of a solid, and (b) the solid shapes given by such cuts. Not all of the names need be identified at

this level. Bisecting a cylinder vertically would give a semicircular prism, but the interesting shape could be noted without necessarily being named. Having said this, children are fascinated by these sorts of words. They will need to know them eventually and so they could be introduced without making a big deal of it. We should, however, have as an objective that children should certainly learn the names of the shapes specified by the National Curriculum and where these shapes occur. They will know some of them, but may be surprised to find for example, a rectangular face cropping up when a cylinder is sliced vertically.

3 A circle is a set of points, all of which are at a specified distance from a centre point. This is quite a difficult concept. Our objective here is only to begin to get some idea that this is the case. Some children may also begin to understand that there is an infinite number of lines of reflective symmetry in a circle or a sphere.

4 We should not be afraid to talk about those shapes which resemble those with which we are dealing. A golf ball is not a sphere, a rolling pin is not a cylinder. The important thing is why not? Our objective here is to see what it is that prevents our shape from having that sort of definition.

5 A further objective is to look at the patterns which can be made with shapes and to refine knowledge about tessellations.

Objectives for supporting areas of the curriculum are not included here. However, it is clear that progression in art would arise, and of course objectives should be identified in language. There are so many of these at this level and they would vary so much with attainments in any class, that it seems best to omit them altogether and leave them to individual teachers.

Content and learning

Introduction

The teacher can tell the children that there will be some exciting work about shapes and ask them to bring in a collection of objects. When these have been supplemented by the teacher's own collection they can be displayed for the children to handle and discuss amongst themselves. It is important to include interesting non-regular shapes: rocks, vegetables, a golf ball, a bell-shaped vase, for example, to promote discussion. After the collection has been established and examined, the teacher can identify, with the children, those shapes with curves in them for further investigation. What can we say about these shapes? What can we do with them? This starting point can be followed by the activities set out below, not necessarily in this order, to meet the mathematical objectives. These activities can be augmented by any others suggested by the class.

Phase 1: Activities

- Drawing circles freehand.
- Experimenting with compasses to make circles.
- Cutting out and folding the circles drawn with compasses or provided by the teacher to explore the length of the radius and diameter at several points in the circles.
- Using circles to see how many lines of symmetry can be drawn.
- Making patterns and overlapping pattern with circles (tissue paper is effective here).
- Tessellating with circles (they do not tessellate but the shapes that the spaces between the circles make can be discussed).
- Trying out tessellation using Islamic patterns and other two-dimensional shapes which include curves. Here one could include activities such as printing and designing dress material or wallpaper.
- Tie dyeing by tying with buttons, noting the fuzzy circular shape and contrasting this with an accordion pleat type result.
- Looking at pictures by artists who use circles in their work (e.g. Kandinsky) and painting pictures of their own.
- Looking at the properties of spheres, cones and cylinders, naming them, naming two-dimensional shapes where there are faces, sorting objects which are 'nearly' cones, spheres and cylinders, discussing why they are not cones, spheres or cylinders and identifying the characteristics of each. Making collections of these objects for labelling and display.
- Looking at what happens when cones, spheres and cylinders are sliced in various ways.
- Printing with sliced spheres and comparing the results to printing with objects which are 'like' sliced spheres such as apples. This could also be done with sliced cones and sliced carrots.
- Making spirals with crêpe paper.

Phase 2: Assessment and consolidation

In phase 1 the normal ongoing assessment will occur. However, as suggested above, there would be specific purposes for assessment which would require time and further planning. To this end, the teacher would return to the original collection of a variety of solid shapes. It is hoped that these would include cubes, cuboids, rectangular and triangular prisms in many sizes. As a new or revision feature, the teacher would introduce making nets for solids. Very often children can make these themselves after being given the opportunity to take hollow 'solids' apart. Children would also be asked to repeat an appropriate selection of the above activities with the new shapes. During these activities, the teacher would check by talking with and observing children, that the relationship between a two-dimensional and a three-dimensional shape was solidly established and point out, where necessary, the connections between this new set of shapes and the shapes with curves. She or he would also check on vocabulary and knowledge of the characteristics of particular shapes.

CONCLUSION

It has been argued that there is much to be gained by teaching a substantial part of the mathematics curriculum in topic work. Suggestions have been made about how mathematics can support topics and topics in mathematics itself, set in the general context of the overall curriculum and of children learning. Earlier we noted that HMI have suggested (DES 1979) that opportunities for dealing with mathematics in thematic work were often missed because teachers had insufficient knowledge of mathematics to identify them. It is not commonly realised outside the profession just how much teachers must know about mathematics to teach young children. Sometimes this is just a case of realising that what is obvious to an adult is obscure when you are little. Sometimes it has to be acknowledged that we need to know a lot about the progress of mathematics to teach young children mathematics well. Luckily, many teachers who did not like mathematics very much when they were at school find that their own interest and knowledge is increased when they begin to teach young children. We hope that some of the things that have been discussed in this chapter will whet the appetites of such teachers. Children in early years seem to enjoy mathematics. It would be an excellent thing for them if we could keep it that way.

Chapter 6

Geography and topic work

To begin this chapter with what is perceived to be wrong with geography in early years topic work could be interpreted as being a rather negative way to assist schools in the process of putting it to rights. On the other hand, it is helpful to identify issues on which staffroom discussions and inset sessions may be based. Along with history, geography has been the subject of serious criticism by HMI in recent surveys of teaching and learning in primary schools (see, for example, *Aspects of Primary Education: The Teaching and Learning of History and Geography*, DES 1989a), wherein it is claimed that in the vast majority of schools surveyed, geography was taught through topic work and satisfactory or good practice was often related to aspects of topic work *other than* geography (and history). Inspection of work related specifically to these subjects showed a far less satisfactory position in the majority of schools.

> Overall standards of work in geography were very disappointing . . . geography was most frequently taught in association with other areas of the curriculum . . . the amount of time allocated to work with a geographical component was rarely adequate . . . in most schools, there was a tendency for geography to lose its distinctive contribution and to become a vehicle for practising skills related to language and art. In contrast the mathematical and scientific potential of geographical skills, in the case of map work and weather observations, was only occasionally exploited.
>
> (DES 1989a)

Criticism was not confined to the area of skills, but also applied to content:

> Work related to other places in the British Isles and the world was limited. The almost total absence of a national and world dimension to the work in many cases highlighted the need for schools to consider a broader perspective.
>
> (DES 1989a)

The survey does, of course, describe and illuminate facets and examples of good practice alongside these and other criticisms, but it is interesting to consider reasons for its negative findings in relation to geography. These include the relatively low status which has traditionally been given to this area of the curriculum, reflected in a poor level or almost complete absence of resources in many schools.

In few schools did the resources reflect the multi-ethnic composition of either the school or society in terms of books, maps, audio and visual materials. There was some evidence to suggest that schools which were most successful in teaching geography also possessed a broad range of resources.

(DES 1989a)

Also, and perhaps of even greater significance, they include the limited understanding by schools of geography's distinctive contribution to young children's learning, coupled with a lack of planning of content to take account of key geographical skills and ideas.

[T]here was rarely a clear rationale for the selection of topics, with little cognizance taken of the age, ability and experience of the pupils. Topics tended to be chosen in an idiosyncratic way by individual teachers, often determined by the television programmes that happen to be available at the time.'

(DES 1989a)

Enough, at this stage, of the negative – yet these are issues well worth bearing in mind as the chapter unfolds into a more positive discussion of the nature and place of geography in Key Stage 1.

At the outset it should be emphasised that the topic work approach is totally appropriate for the inclusion of geographical work at this Key Stage. From the same HMI survey: 'Topic work was an important and integral part of the curriculum in all the schools where there was good practice; it was the major vehicle for promoting geography, history and science.' (DES 1989a).

A cautionary note must be added, however, which is that in the best practice it is essential that a topic has a central and discernible core of geography rather than having rather vague links with a large number of curriculum areas brought about by pursuing a very general theme.

Support for the topic work approach is also reflected in the National Curriculum Order for Geography (DES 1991b) interpreted in *Non-Statutory Guidance* (NCC 1991b) which also emphasises the cautionary note about the need for geography having a central and discernible place in the topic.

In Key Stage 1 and 2, geography may be taught via:

- a broad topic, such as *homes*, covering several subjects, which takes up a substantial time each week for a half term;
- a subject-led topic, such as *weather in different parts of the world*, studied for a more limited period of time.

Topic work planned to take advantage of this overlap [between geography and other National Curriculum subjects] must not rely on contrived links but must provide opportunities for pupils to make realistic connections between subjects.'

(NCC 1991b)

This advice reflects one of the key theses of this chapter, and indeed, the book as a whole, which is that when two or more areas of knowledge are brought together under the umbrella of general topic work, it is essential that the integrity and distinctive characteristics of each are maintained.

The National Curriculum Order for Geography provides a much needed rationale for teaching and learning in the subject, addressing such criticisms as have been mentioned, and giving rise to a number of key issues which will be discussed after a reminder of the main features of the Order. It should be noted that the geography requirements are fundamentally different from those of history, outlined in chapter 3, in so far as geography has no content-specific study units. The designing of topics is entirely a matter for teachers' and schools' discretion, bearing in mind the programmes of study, attainment targets and statements of attainment. Within the programme of study for Key Stage 1 (as for all stages) physical, human and environmental geography are referred to as 'Themes'. As a whole, it outlines five sections, corresponding to attainment targets, which describe what should be taught. These are:

- *Geographical skills*– AT1
- *Places and themes*
- Places– AT2
- Physical geography– AT3
- Human geography– AT4
- Environmental geography– AT5

The programme of study for Key Stage 1 applies to levels 1–3 of levels of attainment. As with other key stages, it is subdivided into a programme of study for all pupils in the key stage and a programme of study for those who are working towards the highest levels of attainment (level 3 in the case of Key Stage 1). Between them, these elements describe the 'matters, skills and processes' that should be taught. An example of this progression, worthy of quote as it will be referred to later, is:

Physical Geography (A11) Pupils should be taught to:
- investigate soil, water and rocks, including sand, and recognise that these materials are part of the natural environment;

- identify water in different forms;
- identify familiar landscape features, including rivers, hills, ponds and woods, and explore different gradients of slope;
- investigate the effects of weather on themselves and their surroundings and recognise seasonal weather patterns.

Pupils working towards level 3 should be taught:
- to identify and describe landscape features, for example, a river, a hill, valley, lake, beach, with which they are familiar;
- the effect of different surfaces and slopes on rainwater when it reaches the ground;
- about weather conditions in different parts of the world, for example, in polar, temperate, tropical desert and tropical forest regions.

(DES 1991b)

The five attainment targets for geography describe the 'knowledge, skills and understanding' which learners are to acquire through the teaching of the programmes of study. They are (as summarised in *Non-Statutory Guidance*):

AT1 *Geographical Skills* – covers the use of maps and field-work techniques.

AT2 *Knowledge and Understanding of Places* – covers the distinctive features, similarities and differences between places in local, regional and international contexts.

AT3 *Physical Geography* – covers: weather and climate, rivers, seas and oceans; landforms; and animals, plants and soils.

AT4 *Human Geography* – covers population, settlements, communications and movements, and economic activities.

AT5 *Environmental Geography* – covers the use and misuse of natural resources, the quality and vulnerability of different environments and the possibilities for protecting and managing environments.

(NCC 1991b)

Each attainment target has ten levels of attainment and, in line with other areas of the National Curriculum, this arrangement covers all four key stages on a continuous scale. Statements of attainment are written to apply to each level.

A number of key points can be teased out of an analysis of the attainment targets. In particular, note should be made that AT1, Geographical Skills, is divided into two elements, namely the use of maps and fieldwork. This attainment target is not intended to be taught in isolation, but to be related to the content of the others. AT2 is concerned with knowledge and understanding of places, and the programmes of study specify places to be taught. In Key Stage 1, learners are required to learn about the local area, a contrasting locality in the UK and a locality beyond the UK.

Localities fitting the last two categories are for individual teachers/ schools to select. AT3, Physical Geography, is divided into four elements: weather and climate (the atmosphere); rivers, river basins, seas and oceans (the hydrosphere); landforms (the lithosphere); and animals, plants and soil (the biosphere). As with AT2, no specific places are identi- fied that are to be studied. Selection should be made to suit individual schemes and overall curriculum plans. AT4, Human Geography, follows a similar pattern. Four divisions of this are population, settlements, com- munications and movements, and economic activities. Again, no set places for study are recommended, although the *Non-Statutory Guidance* makes the useful point that it would be helpful to choose the same places that are selected for work covering attainment targets 2 and 3. Finally, AT5, Environmental Geography, is very closely linked to the National Curriculum's cross-curricular theme of Environmental Education. As such, it highlights a critical dimension of geography teaching, that which is concerned with values, beliefs and issues. 'It is important that pupils take into account conflicting interests and different cultural perspectives when developing an understanding of how people can affect their environment' (NCC 1991b). This is a key dimension to teaching and learning which will be elaborated upon in later discussion. AT5 is sub- divided into three elements, namely the use of and misuse of natural resources; the quality and vulnerability of different environments; and the possibilities for protecting and managing environments.

Before moving away from precise scrutiny of National Curriculum documentation, the crucial relationship between attainment targets and programmes of study must be emphasised. As the programmes of study describe what should be taught to help learners meet the requirements of the attainment targets, which in turn describe the knowledge, skills and understanding which learners are expected to acquire, then it is essential that planning and implementation of schemes and topics takes account of both of these elements.

> Teachers will naturally want to base their planning on the AT's as these describe learning outcomes. However, pupils will only reach the AT's through use of the geographical contexts described in the programmes of study.

> (NCC 1991b)

Again, this key point will be taken up later when organisation and plan- ning are discussed.

Consideration of comments made by Her Majesty's Inspectorate, together with the framework and rationale of the National Curriculum, enables many current issues in early years geography teaching to be teased out. In no particular order of priority, key points which emerge (and which may form a useful agenda for inset discussions) include:

- Geography can be used as a focus for teaching and learning on the nature and dynamics of places, both local and further afield, the spatial relationships involved, the human dimension and environmental impacts and issues. This focus emphasises the distinctive nature of geography which can make its own particular contribution to young children's learning and personal and social development. Also, in the words of the National Curriculum, it 'helps pupils make sense of their surroundings and the wider world'.
- The use of the local environment is a central element of geographical work in primary schools generally, and of early years teaching in particular. This is the all-important starting point or stimulus for development of sound geography and cross-curricular interpretation.
- It is important to encourage the study of localities elsewhere in the United Kingdom and beyond.
- Fieldwork and the process of enquiry in teaching methodologies are essential to geographical education and an integral part of any effective topic or scheme of work, no matter how young the learners. Indeed, progressive attainment in fieldwork and enquiry skills is to be recognised as a component of geography in its own right.
- The context of geography must be established. In other words, it is essential to consider the relationship with and interconnectedness of geographical education with other subject areas. As already mentioned, geography has a distinctive contribution to make to young children's learning and is supportive of learning in other areas of the curriculum. These links should be recognised, respected and planned for.

Rather than continue a discussion in the abstract, these and other related issues will now be considered in context with specific examples of content. Two 'topics in action' will be addressed, the first on mapwork, clearly addressing attainment target 1 as well as aspects of the immediate locality, the second on approaches to looking at distant environments.

TWO TOPICS IN ACTION

Mapwork

No child in school is too young to begin to be introduced to basic elements of mapwork, although in the first two years, skills are likely to be rooted in their immediate surroundings. Topic work planning should take account of the basic elements of mapwork (Catling, 1988) which combine to provide the topic's content. These are:

1 *Perspective*: This presents features in plan form, enables us to see what is hidden from view at ground level.

2 *Position and orientation*: Maps show how various features are related to one another in 'space' and where they are located. From them, we can give directions. Systems of grid referencing enable us to give accurate locations.

3 *Scale*: Maps are scaled-down versions of the real thing. A plan view of a landscape or place is represented on a piece of paper.

4 *Map content*: Content varies from map to map. Some emphasise specific features, e.g. streets, buildings, height of land. Content is dependent on the purpose for which the map is intended and, of course, its scale.

5 *Symbols*: These are used to indicate what is recorded in the map's content. A key is a related feature, necessary so that the map reader can interpret the symbols.

6 *Additional information*: Maps often provide useful information to supplement the content symbols, for example, names of streets, buildings, towns, etc., types of farmland, shops, age of historic sites.

This content serves to help meet the basic aim of the topic expressed in conceptual terms which is to help to develop the children's concepts of space and place, both fundamental to geographical education. The content should also be interpreted within the context of the National Curriculum requirements of AT1, concerned with skills – expressed in the following extract from the programme of study for Key Stage 1.

Geographical Skills

3. Pupils should be taught to:
   * follow directions, including the terms forwards and backwards, up and down, left and right, north, south, east, west;
   * extract information from, and add to, pictorial maps;
   * draw round objects to make a plan, for example, mathematical shapes and household objects;
   * make representations of actual or imaginary places, for example, their own bedroom, a treasure island;
   * identify land and seas on maps and globes;
   * follow a route on a map, for example, a map of the local area or the school produced by a teacher, another adult or pupil;
   * use pictures and photographs to identify features, for example, homes, railways, rivers, hills and to find out about places;
   * observe, describe and record the weather over a short period.
4. Pupils working towards level 3 should be taught to:
   * use the eight points of a compass;
   * make a map of a short route, showing main features in the correct order, for example, from home to the park;
   * use letter and number coordinates to locate features on maps;

- locate their own position and identify features using a large scale map;
- identify features on oblique aerial photographs.

(DES 1991b)

A detailed topic plan can therefore be devised which includes reference to the specific geographical education which forms its central core, expressed in terms of content, concepts and skills, cross-referenced with the relevant attainment targets (notably AT1) and statements of attainment for levels 1–3. It is then appropriate to consider which other areas of the curriculum will be addressed in implementing this plan so that meaningful links are identified and included in planning documentation.

So what might this actually look like in an infant classroom? It is true that formal map work as such is perhaps not relevant to children who have recently entered school. Nevertheless, spontaneous mapping is definitely to be encouraged. These early maps are likely to be pictorial and egocentric. As demonstrated by Piaget and others (1956, 1960) by the age of about 4, children are beginning to understand the locations of objects which surround them in relation to one another, or in a topological sense. Topological cognitive maps (Catling 1978) will be drawn, which contain pictures (e.g. of home, school, trees, church) linked together in some way without the formality of orientation and scale. Such picture maps gradually acquire formality in the sense that connections will be made between objects. For example, roads may be drawn, perhaps in plan form, linking buildings that are still drawn pictorially. There will still be no accuracy of direction, orientation and scale. It is generally believed (Boardman 1983) that by the age of 7, children reach a stage of development in which a 'projective' representation of objects evolves from the topological. Such things as buildings will now be represented in two dimensions rather than as pictures. A child of this age could well be producing something which more closely resembles a 'map' as we know it, with attention to detail, direction, orientation and scale, although these will be far from accurate in most cases. A wide range of classroom tasks will assist in this progression towards formality and accuracy. Children can be encouraged to draw pictorial, spontaneous maps of such things as 'my house and street', 'my route to school', 'where I go to the shops'. Imaginative picture mapping can also arise from story time – many stories lend themselves to drawing journeys or to the reconstruction of places. This is an excellent cross-curricular link with English through story, discussion and vocabulary.

The element of perspective can be developed through a wide range of drawing games and activities. To begin with no direction or scale need be involved. Give the children a sheet of plain paper and ask them to draw around familiar objects which fit on to it – a pencil, ruler, key, building block, toy, etc. What they are actually doing is a basic element of mapwork – representing familiar objects in plan form without any scaling down. A large amount of discussion can be generated by this task. Consider such questions as: What is the *same* about the objects when drawn in this way? (shape, size). What has *changed*? (colour, detail, texture, etc.).

Games can be devised, so that the children draw around objects for their friends to try and identify. They can be coloured in and details added to make the drawings look like the real thing. Progress by asking children to imagine that a little beetle has walked on to their sheet of paper and wants to investigate all of the objects depicted. Draw a path that the beetle may take to visit all of the objects. As the drawings are joined in this way, they have been linked together in space and in the child's mind. This is an important mapwork concept. Activities such as these can extend over several lessons, familiarising children with the idea that a map is a representation of space occupied by objects depicted in plan form and of the spatial relationship between them.

Further activities which the children will enjoy can reinforce the notion of a plan being a 'bird's eye view'. Compare, for example, a plan with an oblique view.

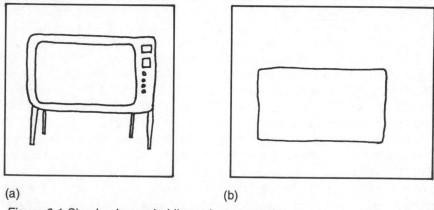

(a)   (b)

Figure 6.1 Simple plan and oblique view comparison

At the simplest level, draw one object in oblique view, e.g. a television set (Fig. 6.1a) and discuss what this would look like when drawn in plan form (Fig. 6.1b). Ask children to say what a bird would see when flying over it. Would it see the programme? There is endless scope for elaboration of this activity as scenes become more complex (Fig. 6.2).

Many scenes of increasing complexity can be drawn for the children to 'match' and colour, and they can be asked to construct their own plans

(a)   (b)

Figure 6.2 Plan and oblique view comparison: more complex scene

from the oblique view. Activities of this kind lead very neatly into discussion on the use of keys. The objects drawn can be colour coded to show an understanding of what matches with what in the two scenes. Boxes can be drawn below the diagrams to be coloured in as a key. This aspect of work also links with the development of skills of symbolic representation. As already mentioned, young children's natural inclination is to draw pictures rather than symbols. Drawing plans from oblique views encourages discussion about suitable ways of representing the 'bird's eye view' of objects ranging from everyday classroom items to the wider world of buildings, trees, railway lines etc. As a progression from activities such as those described, children can be asked to construct their own maps (without accurate scale) and devise their own symbols. A very important question can then be asked: how do other people interpret your symbols? Again, this links to an understanding of the need for a key, and the idea that many published maps (e.g. Ordnance Survey maps) have an agreed pattern of symbols that can easily be recognised. Ideas such as these link skills of map construction with the equally important skills of map reading and interpretation.

As far as scale is concerned, children in the early years in school are surrounded by experience of this without conscious realisation or discussion of the fact. These golden opportunities can be used to raise awareness of scaled down versions of reality. Questions such as 'why is the train-set in the classroom smaller than a real one?' and 'why is the dolls' cutlery smaller than that which we use at lunchtime?' will promote very valuable geographical discussion, linked to the general development of vocabulary and conversation about everyday things. Introduce the formality of scale by asking how we could represent an object which is bigger than the piece of paper we want to draw it on (this will lead on naturally from the 'drawing around familiar objects' activities already described as inevitably some children will have selected items that were bigger than their paper). Initially, concentrate on a scale of half size, done best with pieces of paper or card in the first instance, and then (probably in Year 2) progress to more complex scales and ideas on how we draw such things as our desk, the classroom, the school, the playground. Excellent potential exists for meaningful links with mathematics at this stage. The key idea to be grasped is, for example, that a line 30 cm long will need to be represented by a line 15 cm long on paper. Whilst little formal work can be done in interpreting scales, do introduce children to a variety of published maps, partly as an awareness raising exercise. They will see that not all maps are of the same scale. We have 'large scale maps', and 'small scale maps', some maps show the whole world on a piece of paper, others show only the streets of the locality. As with the use of scale, nursery and infant children are well used to the concept of location of objects in their everyday activities. Plenty of practice can be given of putting models back in the correct place, making sure that apparatus is placed in its correct order, etc. Perhaps a model village could be set out, and then reassembled so buildings and trees are replaced in similar positions. This is very sound early years geography, affording practice in recording locations and in simple plan/map construction. Key vocabulary to be introduced includes 'opposite', 'in front of', 'by the side of', 'behind', 'next to'. The progression of these skills in Key Stage 2 will involve an understanding of grids and coordinates in order to make specific locations explicit. Such skills are linked to an understanding of direction, which in the early years involves familiarity with the vocabulary of 'right', 'left', 'backwards', 'forwards', etc., and an awareness of rotation – of oneself in space. Many opportunities exist for links with PE. Children can move so many paces backwards, forwards, right and left, and move themselves around to face in other directions. Generally, teachers do such things as a matter of routine, perhaps not realising that they are doing basic mapwork or reinforcing the spatial dimensions of everyday life! Formal elements of direction, the points of the compass may, in accordance with National Curriculum guidelines, be introduced with pupils at attainment level 3, beginning with the four cardinal points, north, south, east and west.

A final element of mapwork, that of relief, or height of land, is perhaps the most difficult of all to introduce at a formal level. It is difficult even for adults to appreciate the abstract idea that a certain place is so many metres above the level of the sea and is represented by contour lines. In Key Stage 1 it is perfectly appropriate to reinforce basic vocabulary of relief, such as 'high up', 'low', 'hills', 'steep' and 'gentle', and to show maps which do indicate that some land is higher than others. The relief of the locality can be discussed; perhaps some children have to walk up or down hills to get to school or to the shops, and some may visit hilly or mountainous areas, which can be described in terms of their being 'high up', with views 'over' other land which is 'lower'.

It is an interesting observation that very few early years classrooms seem to have a good range of maps on display, perhaps because of the belief that formal map interpretation is for later years of schooling. On the other hand, how valuable it is to have the widest possible variety of maps and plans (including aerial photographs) for children to observe. Even if the formality is beyond their conceptual capacity, Key Stage 1 children will gain a great deal from awareness that various forms of map exist. It is perfectly appropriate to display as many forms of map-style representation as possible, including maps of the world, large scale maps of the locality and school environment, street plans of your town or village, A–Z type maps, and Ordnance Survey maps. Add to these, regular displays of the children's own maps and maps of imaginary places.

This detailed example of developing mapwork skills in the chapter has been included for two purposes: first, to give a number of practical ideas which hopefully will be of use for anyone planning topics on this subject; second, to demonstrate that whilst mapping is an example of education which is specifically geographical and therefore needs to be addressed in its own right as a discernible and critical area of learning, it can be linked in a meaningful way to other areas of the curriculum (notably mathematics, PE, English and environmental education) and, to a large extent, it arises spontaneously out of traditional good practice in the early years classroom. It is an excellent example of how the skills of geography (in this case graphicacy) can contribute to the general intellectual development of children in the first three years in school.

Distant lands

So we now turn to the second example of a 'topic in action', which aims to illustrate a range of other issues on a much broader scale. One of the key points emerging from HMI views and the National Curriculum Order is the 'challenge to parochialism' and the need for children to learn the geography of places beyond the immediate environment of the school. For Key Stage 1, this includes study of another locality in the UK and of a place beyond. These places can be used as appropriate for work towards the attainment targets on Physical Geography, Human Geography and Environmental Geography. The following discussion focuses to a far greater extent on issues which are important to address at staff planning meetings and on 'how to go about it' rather than on 'what to teach' as the National Curriculum gives specific guidelines on the latter (DES 1991b).

Young children's background knowledge of distant environments is an important consideration when planning work on them, although perhaps the word 'knowledge' is not the most accurate one to use. Children have an ever-increasing incidental contact with places around the world through personal contacts, package holidays and from a wide variety of media. Inevitably, they build up a 'mental map' or images of such places which to a large extent may be blurred or false. Television, radio, books and videos are all very powerful influences. Children's television programmes certainly acknowledge that the 'rest of the world' exists through reference to foreign foods, homes, environments, animals, etc., and by having contributors or presenters from overseas or parts of the UK with distinct accents. A story such as *A Bear Called Paddington* (Bond 1976) helps children to learn that Peru exists – although no doubt they think one always goes there via Paddington railway station! It should be stressed that the word 'distant' does not necessarily mean thousands of miles overseas, and so the National Curriculum recommendation to teach about a contrasting area of the United Kingdom is to be welcomed. To a 5-year-old growing up in the centre of Newcastle upon Tyne, the farmlands and tin mines of Cornwall are as distant as any other place. An interesting discussion on the blurred knowledge contained within children's 'world inside their heads' is provided by Bale (1987). He draws attention to various research findings on both the quantity and quality of information which children possess of places beyond their immediate environment. As well as factual errors, attention is drawn to the dangers of stereotyping and ethnocentricity that result from media reports. Fyson (1984) reports a word association test with primary age children in Wokingham, England. Results showed that the words most commonly associated with 'Africa' were 'lions', 'heat', 'snakes', 'elephants', 'trees', 'tigers', 'palm trees' and 'black people'. Such words conjure up images of the exotic and the excitement of the land, and are far removed from the realities of racism, apartheid, poverty, mineral resources and large cities which are typical of some parts of Africa today.

The development of attitudes over time is another related point to consider.

> The 7-year-old is more likely to think in terms of absolutes (e.g. good – bad) whereas the 11 year-old begins to see shades of relationships.
>
> (Bale 1987)

> In the primary school the study of places should certainly take account of younger children's curiosity and relative openness.
>
> (ILEA 1981)

These factors cannot of course be separated from racism.

> The inferiority of people from countries other than our own is implicitly communicated by a vast range of media including comics, films, television programmes, books and newspapers.
>
> (Bale 1987)

This is a crucial issue to be considered when approaching and planning the study of foreign lands in geography teaching, especially as mis-information, the origins of racial ideas and bias can easily arise from a teacher's genuine ignorance of particular facts about a place. The argument being developed is clearly paradoxical. The appropriate starting point for geographical studies is 'where the children are', building upon existing knowledge and concepts, yet as pointed out, to a certain extent these will be incomplete, erroneous or even biased. Indeed, children's views of the world and mental maps are essential building bricks. Good practice involves making the foundations as solid as possible. A great challenge in the planning of distant lands topic work is to provide learners with accurate information and experience that is exciting enough to capture their imagination and the desire to learn more, leading to an appreciation of environmental conditions which are different from our own, and building up a more accurate and complete picture of the place being studied.

Key issues involved in this challenge are:

- Starting points – the selection of places, accepting that you cannot study the whole world in Key Stage 1!
- What questions should the children to be asking and investigating about distant places?
- How can we avoid the stereotyping and racist overtones which may emerge?
- How can work be made relevant to the children's own lives?

A little more will be said about each of these.

Selection of places cannot be divorced from a more general discussion on planning the curriculum (see below) so that a good range of places are studied across Key Stage 1 (with appropriate 'bridges' into Key Stage 2). *Non-Statutory Guidance* (NCC, 1991b) recommends that places should be selected to:

- provide a balanced spread of knowledge about places around the world, enabling pupils to relate newly encountered places to those already known;
- cover a range of scales – local, regional, national and international;
- reflect current interest around the world;
- provide opportunities for the study of ATs 1, 3, 4, 5.

When teaching about distant places teachers should avoid possible pitfalls such as:

- portraying an outdated or stereotyped image of places and people; (for example, modern life for the Inuit, as they prefer to be called, may involve working for the oil industry and living in houses rather than hunting and living in temporary shelters such as igloos);

- giving a limited view of a country, (for example, that Sri Lanka only produces tea);
- using biased material about a country, (for example, material which portrays only the attractions of living, working or travelling in a country).

(NCC, 1991b)

It would seem sensible for schools, when working out curriculum plans and topics bearing in mind the above advice, to make a list of criteria for selection of places so that a balance is achieved. Such criteria might well include:

- Study of places of which teachers have personal experience. How useful it is to be able to talk knowledgeably about distant lands, having travelled there, lived and eaten there, viewed the scenery and talked with indigenous people. Objects, souvenirs and photographs in a personal collection will be valuable teaching aids. If a member of staff has lived in a country for a period of time, rather than visited it for a speedy holiday in one resort, then so much the better.
- Study of places which the children, parents or friends have personal experience of. Once again, souvenirs and photographs will be readily available, as will stories of 'real life' in the land. A class is far more likely to be motivated by the study of somewhere that one of its members can speak of, than somewhere selected at random.
- Study of places where school contacts and links can be developed. How valuable it would be to the topic if, for example, the children can exchange letters, photographs, writing, weather statistics and news stories with children who live in the distant place. Do seek out contacts in both foreign and distant UK locations. A school in London, for example, could 'twin' with one in the uplands of Wales. An ongoing school link will be much more productive than a short term exchange set up for the duration of a single topic.
- Study of 'topical' places – that is, ones which are receiving plenty of media coverage that can be a source of information, cuttings, photographs and discussion. Such places range from those at war to those with happier current events, e.g. the World Cup or Olympic Games.

By implementing the above suggested set of valid criteria for selection of places to encounter, it is likely that a good range is achieved, and that there is a balance between places studied by the school regularly (with a wide range of resources built up for the purpose) and those studied on a 'one off' basis for some good reason.

The National Curriculum Order and *Non-Statutory Guidance* gives helpful advice on the content of teaching and learning, what questions should be asked, and the importance of the enquiry method. This cannot be separated in discussion from the issues of bias/stereotyping and making work relevant to the children's own lives. Views have already been given and quoted from the NCC on the need to avoid fostering the development of false and biased images of places. One way of achieving this aim (whilst acknowledging that to a certain extent some degree of bias and 'blurred' knowledge in young children is probably unavoidable) is to relate coverage of distant places back to the locality and the children's personal experiences. This has two powerful benefits psychologically, viz:

- It helps the children identify more easily with the topic, place or people under consideration; and
- it helps them to understand the interdependence of the modern world.

If young people can feel a part of this world and appreciate its links with their own, they may be less likely to view it as totally alien, exotic or remote from their own reality. Furthermore, they may be less likely to interpret it as 'better' or 'worse' than their own 'world'.

In many ways, this point emphasises the natural and very important links that geographical education has with the cross-curricular dimension of multi-cultural education. The study of distant lands is an ideal way of promoting the permeation of learning about other cultures, traditions, beliefs and values.

> Multicultural education seeks to prepare pupils for life in a world where they will live and work with people of different cultures, religions, languages and ethnic origins. Geography's role is to help pupils build an informed and balanced view of the world and their place in it.
>
> (NCC 1991b)

The study of distant lands also emphasises the critical links with the cross-curricular theme of environmental education, a point made earlier in the chapter when referring to AT5, Environmental Geography. This attainment target highlights the importance of learning about conflicting interests and different cultural values, which can be addressed in context when learning about distant places.

A full cross-referencing between AT5 and the guidelines for Environmental Education can be made by consulting *Curriculum Guidance 7* (NCC, 1990).

Space does not allow a detailed discussion on strategies for developing values education from geographical starting points, but any topic plan should acknowledge the critical role of this dimension of learning and teachers should bear in mind the importance of the developing attitudes, beliefs and values in the minds of their young learners.

Thus it is important to relate coverage of life in distant lands back to children's personal life experiences, emotions and feelings. How do we do it? In the first three years of school there can be no better answer than 'make it real', by using tangible objects, the concrete, that which is part of their own reality and meets the challenge of motivation. Three things readily spring to mind which meet this challenge, which are rich enough to capture young imagination, these are:

- animals
- plants
- food.

As a general rule, infants are interested in and enthusiastic about all three! Each will make a very worthwhile general topic that has a distant environment as its major focus, although many other general themes would be appropriate, including homes, clothes and holidays. Bear in mind that the above are recommended as exciting *starting points* – and as the topic unfolds, various aspects of the foreign place will be explored. The point being made is that the foreign environment should not be irrelevant and there must be some point of contact between the pupils and the topic. Actual objects from a country attract attention and will speedily motivate. They are the 'specimens' of geography and have the same value that artefacts have in history, as discussed in chapter 3. Perhaps one object could start the topic, or an 'interest table' could be built up – with an accumulation of souvenirs/artefacts that tell of the land, its people and environment. Stories, maps, photographs, travel brochures and news cuttings could add supplementary interest and background information.

To complete the discussion on distant lands, perhaps one example would be useful, selected from the categories named above. Take an avocado pear as a starting point. What a wonderful talking point this is, and one readily available in most supermarkets. Children could go on a shopping expedition to study fruits and vegetables available from distant lands, or the teacher could provide it as an 'interesting object'. The avocado is also known as the 'alligator pear' because of its alligator-like skin. It originates from Central America. Talk with the class about the origins of its name, the texture of its skin and general appearance, stimulating vocabulary and oral language work. It can be identified as a pear-shaped fruit. Then investigate the inside of it, noting the contrast with the outside. Dark green to purple tough skin covers an oily, soft, pale green flesh. Pursue links with science attainment targets: grow the stone in the centre of the fruit, experiment with lemon juice by observing how this prevents the flesh from discolouring when exposed to the light; taste the fleshy fruit. The key questions can then be posed:

- Where do avocados grow?
- Where did they originate?

These lead on to a wide range of supplementary questions and perhaps a major topic on Mexico, where the avocado features extensively in traditional dishes. Investigations might go along these lines:

- What is the weather like where avocados grow?
- What are the names of countries where they grow?
- Who grows them?
- What does the plant look like?
- Why are they grown?
- How are they harvested?
- Who buys them?
- How do they travel to importing lands?
- How are they used in native dishes?

Prepare a dish in the classroom using avocados. Guacamole, a well known Mexican dip, is simple

Guacamole

You will need:
2 tomatoes
4 avocados
4 tablespoons lemon juice
2 teaspoons salt
1 small onion, skinned and chopped
3 cloves garlic, crushed
2 teaspoons chilli powder

What to do:
1 Skin and chop the tomatoes
2 Remove peel and stones of avocados
3 Mash avocados with the lemon juice
4 Stir in the salt, chopped tomato, onion, garlic and chilli powder
5 Spoon into a serving bowl and serve with Mexican tortilla chips for authenticity (available from delicatessens or large supermarkets) or crisps.

The above quantity is sufficient to allow a good taste for each class member.

The potential for links with science continues to be extensive, including discussion on the use of spices in foods, changing textures and flavours and the importance of food in our lives. Ideally, prepare this dish as part of a wider topic on Mexico, which investigates costumes, customs, festivals and general ways of life of people who live there. From a tangible starting point, a colourful and exciting geographical topic can be developed. Referring back to the suggested criteria for selecting topics, perhaps it should be explained that this example was chosen because the author of this chapter has visited Mexico and has a wealth of personal experience, supplementary objects and ideas to make the topic exciting and worthwhile. Nevertheless, its ideas could be adapted for any foreign food item available in this country, which gives plenty of scope for selection. If ideas fail, why not start at the Greek, Indian or Chinese takeaway!

PLANNING AND RESOURCES

From practical examples, we now turn to the more general issues of planning and resourcing topic work in geography. Organisation and planning should take account of a whole school and class curriculum plan as well as details of individual topics or other approaches to teaching. School staff will need to discuss:

- how much time is to be allocated to geography-based topics/when they are to fit into the overall curriculum plan;
- whether the topic work approach is to be supplemented by teaching specific skills or content of geography in their own right at any stage;
- the overall balance of links between geography-based topics and other areas of the curriculum – this can, of course, only be done in context when individual topics are designed;
- arrangements for assessment, record-keeping and evaluation of schemes/topics/the plan as a whole;
- availability of an appropriate range of resources.

The school plan will need to cover the whole of the key stage and make provision for 'bridging' with Key Stage 2. It should bear in mind the agreed criteria for selecting places to study, and the overall balance of attainment targets and grouping of statements of attainment. There is scope for a wide range of decisions, as schools have freedom to make choices about places to be studied, how geographical work will be linked across the curriculum and how the various elements of the programme of study will be combined into well-integrated topics. As part of this decision-making process, the interrelationship of topics must be considered. Indeed, it is only through careful linking that the programmes of study and attainment targets will be covered in a coherent way. *Non-Statutory Guidance* makes the key point that although topics need to have a distinct focus, links between them (and with other parts of the curriculum) can be made in a number of worthwhile ways:

- Topics can be linked to give a unifying theme to a year's work.
- Topics can be taught so that they draw on knowledge and understanding acquired in previous topics.

- The timing of a topic should take account of other parts of the curriculum.
- Topics should show how the attainment targets are related.

(NCC 1991b)

Topics in year 1 (and indeed with reception children) could be centred around the children themselves, with their own life experiences being the unifying element (my family, my home, how I get to school, what I wear, what I eat, etc.). It seems an obvious point that topics should draw on knowledge and understanding of previous topics, however, we frequently see young learners lurching in a rather haphazard way from 'Growing things' to 'Christmas' to 'Water' to 'Castles' or whatever. In geography, perhaps more than any other curriculum area, there is ample opportunity to build upon knowledge and skills acquired in topics relating to the local environment in a structured and progressive way, gradually moving onwards and 'outwards' into study of distant and contrasting places. A simple progression from a topic on 'My home' to 'Food/shopping' allows for the progressive introduction of content on distant lands through foreign food items, as developed in the 'avocado' example. Topics should be planned in many ways like a jigsaw puzzle, in that they fit together and reinforce previous learning, gradually building up the overall picture of geographical learning.

Opportunities for links with other areas of the curriculum will inevitably be more obvious and extensive in some topics than in others. Again, it is not enough to leave these to chance or even to acknowledge their existence. Careful planning should include decisions on such matters as whether, for example, scale should be introduced first in mathematics or in geography and at what stage and in what topics this will be reinforced. A simple beginning to this planning task could involve making a list of the content of a broad topic, showing subjects with obvious links:

Food

Subject	Content
Geography, science	What I eat, my favourite foods
Geography	Where I buy my food
Geography, mathematics	Location of food shops in my neighbourhood
Geography, science	Where the food comes from and how it is grown
Geography, technology, economic understanding	Who grows it? The work of a farmer
Geography	Types of farm
Geography, science	The importance of weather and soil for growing food etc.

Similar analysis could then be done for the key concepts and skills of the topic, teasing out those which are specific to geographical education and those which are essentially cross-curricular. Finally, opportunities for cross-curricular development of attitudes, and values, could be identified. Elaboration on this planning could lead to a matrix showing cross links of these elements, not just with broad subject headings but with specific attainment targets where appropriate. The implications for the timing of the teaching of these can then be cor..idered.

Topics and links between topics should have and show a clear understanding of how the attainment targets in geography are related and, indeed, linked to the programmes of study. Several localities could be studied at any one time in order to cover physical, human and environmental geography, or one place may allow for successful integration of these elements, that is, the teasing out of the all important links between them. This aspect of the discussion cannot be separated from the importance of progression, for presumably it is only through gradual extension of content and building up of an increasing complexity of skills and understanding that learners will come to understand such links. Progression has been defined by the National Curriculum Geography Working Group as:

- gradual extension of content to include different places, environments, human activities and physical processes;
- increasing the scale of the place studies from localities, regions and countries, to international and global;
- increasing complexity of the phenomena studied and tasks set;
- use of more generalised knowledge and abstract ideas;
- increasing precision required in practical and intellectual tasks;
- increasing awareness and understanding of social, political and environmental issues involving different attitudes and values.

Planning needs to take account of what and how best to teach so that learners are working towards the next level of attainment. Perhaps the best way of approaching this is to group statements of attainment which have content linked through the topic in the sequence in which they could be introduced in the topic, cross-referencing this plan with content from the programme of study which gives specific guidance as to what pupils working towards the highest attainment level in the key stage should be doing. In practice, this could mean that all children study a general topic on water, learning about it in its different forms and investigating what it looks like in the landscape, perhaps studying a pond or river in the locality. They could then go on to investigate how weather affects water in the landscape (rainwater fills up ponds, causes rivers to flow faster, etc.) with opportunities for level 3 learners to pay attention to different surfaces and slopes and how these affect rainwater when it reaches the ground. Statements of attainment have thus been grouped:

Level	Statement of attainment
1	recognise . . . water . . . and understand it is part of the environment
2	recognise weather patterns identify the forms in which water occurs in the environment
3	describe what happens to rainwater when it reaches the ground

Such grouping allows for progression and takes account of the relevant part of the programme of study. It also has a specific geographical context which can be linked to a progressive study of places, from local through to global. Furthermore, it assists in the processes of record-keeping and assessment, which are, at least in part, about gathering evidence to monitor children's progress in each attainment target. If progression is built into planning, then the task of gathering and interpreting this evidence should be fairly straightforward. Evidence of achievement derived from observation of children at work, talking with them, questioning, listening and assessing materials produced by them can be analysed in the context of the grouped series of statements of attainment.

Geographical education in the early years requires a wide variety of teaching methods with great emphasis on the enquiry approach. Giving knowledge directly, creative activities, questioning, group and individual tasks, IT, use of stories/drama/role play, books, maps and other secondary resources all have their part to play. Yet if asked to single out the most important approach to teaching and learning which characterises well-executed geographical topics, then fieldwork would be the answer. To many, this term no doubt conjures up images of mountains, walking boots and backpacks . . . but no child in school is too young to have a wide variety of learning tasks set in the outdoors, beginning of course, with the school playground and its immediate environment. All work outside the classroom both uses and extends the world with which young children are familiar, and if trips further afield, into the neighbourhood and beyond, can be organised, then so much the better. Ideally, year 2 children should have opportunities to visit and investigate contrasting environments, perhaps a farm if the school is in an inner city area, or a shopping complex/town centre if the school is in a rural community. The inclusion of fieldwork activities should certainly be addressed in all school curriculum plans and policy documents for the teaching of geography.

Teaching and learning will not be possible without resources – an obvious statement – and one, which again, should be the focus of attention in school planning discussions. As mentioned early in this chapter, lack of resources for teaching geography was a key issue highlighted in the HMI survey (DES 1989a), linked to the relatively low status which this subject has seemingly had. With current pressures on schools' budgets the acquisition of a wide range of useful materials is a daunting prospect.

Yet in ways similar to those discussed in the chapter concerned with history, it is a relatively simple task for individual teachers to make collections of useful items. Two examples are obvious:

• Make a collection of maps of various scales, sizes and uses. Consult the local tourist information centre and travel agents, look out for maps in papers and magazines and try to acquire a range of published maps, e.g. an Ordnance Survey map of the local area, world map, A–Z.
• Make collections of objects/illustrative material from distant places you visit. When abroad, or in distant parts of the UK, seek out photographs, posters, examples of local craft work, tapes of authentic music, items of national dress (or pictures of), details of special festivals and customs and traditional foods. Sketch or photograph homes and people.

If every staff member assembles (at no huge expense!) collections of this kind, then the school as a whole would have a wealth of material which could be drawn upon.

The following checklist may be helpful for schools or curriculum co-ordinators setting about the task of building up a range of resources for use in infant geography teaching.

People
• Make a list of staff and contacts of people who have visited distant lands who would be prepared to come and talk about them.
• Make a list of people in the local community, perhaps elderly people who would talk about aspects which have changed through time, or specialist workers (policeman, shopkeeper, vicar) who are knowledge-able about specific buildings, places or jobs in the area.

Places
• Make an inventory of places in the locality and further afield which are of particular geographical interest for fieldwork, with a note of opening hours/special features, if appropriate.

Maps
• Collect together as wide a range as possible. Also, globes, atlases, air photographs. Local newspaper offices often have air photographs available. Local studies sections of the library usually have maps and photographs which can be copied. Ordnance Survey maps can be ordered from Trade Relations (Sales Division), Ordnance Survey, Romsey Road, Maybush, Southampton SO9 4DH.

Books and written sources
• Reference books about themes/topics, e.g. food, homes, also about distant places, world issues, festivals and customs. Newspaper cuttings, tourist brochures, leaflets, wallcharts. Stories set in distant places or about journeys. Recipe books from around the world.

Illustrative material
- Photographs, posters (seek the goodwill of travel agents), slides, filmstrips.

Music
- Collect tapes/records of music from distant places, pictures or examples of their traditional musical instruments.

Mechanical
- IT microcomputers and software, cameras, television programmes, radio programmes, videos of distant lands, films.

Miscellaneous
- Specialist equipment, e.g. for weather recording, pond dipping, soil studies.
- Models, e.g. landscape models, stream channels.
- Objects, e.g. examples of clothing, local craft work from distant places, menus from foreign restaurants.

Much of the above will need very careful selection, and distinction should be made between that which is appropriate for the children to read and use and that which is teacher resource material for study and appropriate interpretation. Both have a place in the school's collection.

In conclusion, there can be little doubt that early years geography teaching is at an exciting stage in its development. Today, perhaps more than ever before, we have a clear focus and rationale which will be used as a baseline for progress in developing sound curriculum plans and strategies for teaching and learning the subject. Cynics would say how good it is that we now *have* some early years geography teaching! We do not share this cynicism, rather the view that many aspects of good practice which have characterised infant education for a very long time are now being *interpreted* and used as a clearly stated focus for developing an area of the curriculum which has traditionally taken a 'back seat' in terms of priority.

The key to success in this task is well-planned topic work – that which recognises and respects the specific contribution which geography can make to the overall development and education of a young learner – and that which addresses in a systematic and progressive way the meaningful links with other selected areas of the curriculum. We do not suggest that this task is easy, but a major advantage has to be that geographical learning has begun long before a child arrives in school. The huge challenge is to build upon and help make sense of children's ongoing experiences of space and place, and of the 'world' as it exists to them.

Chapter 7

Cross-curricular issues and topic work

On first appearance, it may seem curious that a separate (albeit short) chapter is included in the middle of this book on cross-curricular issues, whilst a number of National Curriculum foundation subjects are denied their 'own' chapter through constraints of space. Furthermore, a false impression could well be given that we view cross-curricular matters as a 'special kind of subject' or an appendage to be 'tacked on' to the delivery of core and foundation subjects.

This is not the case. A number of cross-curricular issues are referred to and discussed in context within other chapters of the book; for example, the dimension of multi-cultural education is incorporated into the section on teaching about other cultures and distant places in the geography chapter. The purpose of including a separate discussion of cross-curricular matters is twofold: First, it provides an overview of what is meant by the term 'cross-curricular issues' and considers their place in the curriculum as a whole. Second, it allows us to take a specific example of a theme not addressed elsewhere in the book and to use this to discuss approaches to organisation, teaching and learning of cross-curricular elements, which are, after all, part of the whole curriculum.

Having made the clear statement that cross-curricular issues are not an appendage to be 'tacked on' to the rest of learning, this point will be developed. In many instances in our experience, they are indeed perceived as being peripheral to the main focus of organising the curriculum for teaching and learning.

Under the general umbrella of cross-curricular issues (Table 7.1) are the three elements of skills, dimensions and themes which permeate the curriculum as a whole. These are elaborated upon in Curriculum Guidance 3 (NCC 1990).

> They are the ingredients which tie together the broad education of the individual and augment what comes from the basic curriculum. . . .
> Dimensions such as a commitment to providing equal opportunities for all pupils, and a recognition that preparation for life in a

Table 7.1 Cross-curricular issues of the National Curriculum

Skills	Dimensions	Themes
Communication	Equal opportunities	(i) Economic and industrial understanding
Numeracy	Gender issues	(ii) Careers education and guidance
Study	Multi-cultural perspectives	(iii) Health education
Problem-solving		(iv) Education for citizenship
Personal and social		(v) Environmental education

Source: NCC (1990)

multi-cultural society is relevant to all pupils, should permeate every aspect of the curriculum.

(NCC 1990)

There are of course, a wide range of skills which can be developed in a progressive and coherent way across the curriculum provided that adequate planning and assessment of these is undertaken. It is essential that topics are planned with the progressive development of such skills in mind.

All these skills are transferable, chiefly independent of content and can be developed in different contexts across the whole curriculum. . . .

Teachers will need to locate cross-curricular skills in their schemes of work for each key stage as part of the school's planned programme for skills development.

(NCC 1990)

The planned inclusion of progressive skills teaching through topic work is, of course, a key theme permeating this book as a whole. It is essential that the inclusion of cross-curricular skills in topics is co-ordinated and monitored with the same degree of rigour as the inclusion of subject specific skills (e.g. graphicacy in geography teaching).

Finally, the general umbrella of cross-curricular issues includes five initial themes, considered to be essential parts of the whole curriculum. These are economic and industrial understanding, careers education and guidance, health education, education for citizenship and environmental education.

The themes have in common the ability to foster discussion of questions of values and belief; they add to knowledge and understanding and they rely on practical activities, decision making and the inter-relationship of the individual and the community. . . .

It must remain open to schools to decide how these themes are encompassed within the whole curriculum.

(NCC 1990)

Probably the main way in which cross-curricular themes differ from dimensions, is that they have a substantial body of knowledge and understanding in their own right, incorporating the 'values, belief' component mentioned above. The aims and components of each theme are published in depth in the NCC Series of Curriculum Guidance booklets numbers 4–8 (NCC 1990)

Clearly, space within the chapter does not allow for a detailed account of all cross-curricular themes. Thus one is selected for more detailed attention – environmental education. Through this example, it is hoped to show how cross-curricular elements can indeed go some way towards providing a unifying element for the curriculum as a whole, thus having a key place in the topic work approach to organisation. Guidance for the teaching of this theme is published in *Curriculum Guidance 7* (NCC 1990).

As an officially recognised cross-curricular theme, environmental education must be regarded as part of every pupil's entitlement. It is not a statutory subject in its own right, but, in line with all themes, it must be viewed as being complementary to and permeating all of the core and foundation subjects. The very nature and location of cross-curricular themes suggests that in the National Curriculum we do not necessarily have a straitjacket of subject compartmentalisation. Rather, we have the opportunity within a prescribed framework to promote a sound and well-researched entitlement which is delivered as a coherent whole.

No single approach to the organisation of the curriculum or teaching methodology for environmental education or any other theme is recommended. Indeed, it is believed that a variety of approaches is best utilised. The NCC (1990) identifies five possible timetabling arrangements for the inclusion of cross-curricular themes, namely:

A Taught through National Curriculum and other subjects.
B Whole curriculum planning leading to blocks of activities (e.g. a series of subject-based topics lasting for varying periods of time).
C Separately timetabled themes.
D Taught through separately timetabled personal and social education.
E Longblock timetabling (e.g. activity week).

Clearly, arrangements A and B are those most likely to be used in Key Stage 1. Topics may be subject based, incorporating cross-curricular issues, or the actual focus of a topic could be taken from one of the cross-curricular themes such as environmental education. 'Cross-curricular themes are not necessarily synonymous with the themes or topics currently in use in primary schools and will more often be identified as threads running through them and through subjects' (NCC 1990).

Of all the themes, environmental education is probably the one which has more areas of content or starting points which could well be used as the basis for the development of a general topic. *Curriculum Guidance 7* identifies such areas of knowledge and understanding of the environment and it is interesting to note that within this publication, they are referred to as 'topics'. 'For the most part, these topics will be taught through subjects of the National Curriculum, and in particular through the attainment targets and programmes of study for science, technology, geography and history' (NCC 1990). The named topics are:

- Climate
- Soils, rocks and minerals
- Water
- Materials and resources, including energy
- Plants and animals
- People and their communities
- Building, industrialisation and waste

There are extensive possibilities for classroom interpretation of these topics, and the following case study is intended to illuminate ways of approaching environmental education in practice.

WAVERLEY CROSS SCHOOL

Miss Mann's class of 6–7-year-old children from Waverley Cross School undertook a series of visits to an environmental education day visits centre in the heart of a large industrial city. The centre has classroom facilities and a variety of habitats and opportunities for environmental studies including magnificent gardens, an orchard, greenhouses, poultry pens, a pond, woodland, hedgerows and a meadow. An advisory teacher based at the centre works with visiting class teachers to plan and organise field experiences and to supervise the tasks of visiting pupils. The approach to and extent of school-based follow-up work as a result of visits to the field centre is a matter for individual class teachers to decide and organise. During their field visits, Miss Mann's children gained a wealth of general outdoor experiences, and focused in particular on studies of fruits and vegetables, and then woodland birds.

Back in their classroom, seated in mixed ability working groups, they set about a wide variety of tasks relating to their first hand experiences, observations, and items brought back to school. Samples of fruits and vegetables led to the development of an integrated topic on food. Figure 7.1 illustrates the range of activities covered in the topic.

Following on from this initial topic, the class studied bird life (and its food) at the field centre. This new sub-topic was clearly linked to and developed out of the main topic – both in its planning and in the minds of the children. Various species of birds seen around the centre were noted and identified. They were observed through binoculars, recorded pictorially and graphically, painted and sketched. Their habits were researched from posters and library books and particular notice was taken of feeding patterns. Birds of both fact and fantasy were painted and modelled in papier mâché, frieze boards became 'aviaries', and elaborate food chain mobiles were constructed to suspend from the classroom ceiling. Further units of related study included feathers, migration and nesting.

Science
- Edible plant parts: classification of root, stem, leaf, fruit, flowers, seed
- Cutting cross-sections and microscopic examinations
- Food ingredients
- Food as an energy source
- The human digestive system
- Conditions necessary for plant growing
- Cookery
- Food chains

Maths
- Prices of foods
- Costing a menu

Art
- Colour and texture of fruits and vegetables
- Root and stem prints
- Cross-sectional drawing of fruits and roots
- Food collages

FOOD

History
- Food through the ages

English
- Stories, poems and rhymes about food
- Imaginative stories and food description – fantasy foods
- Writing about favourite foods and disliked foods
- Menu design
- If people became food .... creative stories

Geography
- Foods from distant lands, importance of climate in agriculture
- Farming systems
- Soils and soil types
- Ethnic dishes

Health Education
- Food hygiene
- Need for a balanced diet

Figure 7.1 Food: a topic web of activities based on first-hand environmental experiences

An analysis of this topic indicates that a number of the significant principles pertaining to good quality topic work have been adhered to. As a whole, whilst based on the theme of environmental education, the topic covers a number of key curriculum areas, notably science, mathematics, English, art and geography. Links with these areas are meaningful. It does not attempt to include other foundation subjects that have no immediate or obvious connection for the sake of 'dragging them in'. Secondly, the topic has certain areas of environmental education as its unifying element. It also takes account of meaningful links with other cross-curricular issues, notably health education and education for citizenship. Cross-curricular matters thus have a genuine role to play in bringing together elements of learning. Thirdly, the topic as a whole is not pursued to the point of exhaustion. A new sub-topic is introduced while the children remain motivated and eager to pursue their field studies.

Within this classroom, the teacher believes that a high level of individualisation of learning is vitally important for developing children's ability to work independently and autonomously. Many classroom tasks reflect this view. A large amount of group work also takes place, encouraging collaborative work where children listen to and learn from each other. Because of this approach to child organisation, the class teacher inevitably has a limited amount of time to spend with an individual child or with a small group. The classroom space is organised in 'seating groups', where a number of children sit around adjoining desks. This is a flexible arrangement in that it allows children to work individually and to join in group discussions as and where appropriate. Generally the children are in self-chosen friendship groups. The teacher's approach to learning incorporates key elements of well-planned topic work including the integration of teaching sessions and the minimal use of timetabling.

The key argument put forward by Waverley Cross School for this method of organisation of time and curriculum is that there is flexibility for the pupils to choose how much time is to be spent on an activity, thus encouraging a significant level of responsibility for their own work. Also, teachers in this school believe that there is an increase in the pupils' intrinsic motivation to address tasks, resulting from the fact that to a large extent they have control over and involvement in their own learning. Subject areas of the curriculum tend to be fully integrated in a topic throughout the week with environmental experiences as a frequent starting point for investigation and development. This gives the cross-curricular theme a high profile in the curriculum as a whole. Individuals tend to have their own cross-disciplinary tasks arising from field centre visits as opposed to the whole class undertaking similar, subject-based work. In short, this classroom demonstrates an array of evidence for explicit planning for integration of work through topics based on the field centre visits. The visits are viewed as the beginning of integrated investigation and enquiry rather than as a subject-related end product in itself.

The topic described raises a number of important questions:

- Lively and exciting as this school's work appears to be, to what extent was it planned? (Or did it just happen?)
- What were the details of this planning? (What learning was to be achieved? What attainment targets to be met?)
- How was the proposed learning assessed?
- How were the results accomplished with the stringent time constraints of the National Curriculum?

These key questions will be addressed in general rather than in school-specific terms, although it must be emphasised that the hallmark of Waverley Cross School's success in this particular topic was its meticulous attention to planning and organisational detail at every stage. Classroom activities were carefully based upon and evolved out of (in a context-matched and progressive way) the children's first hand experiences of learning in, for and about the environment.

Planning for the inclusion of environmental education in the curriculum needs to take account of these three linked components:

- education about the environment (that is, basic knowledge and understanding of the environment);
- education for the environment (concerned with values, attitudes and positive action for the environment); and
- education in or through the environment (that is, using the environment as a resource with emphasis on enquiry and investigation and pupils' first hand experiences).

Because of the interrelated nature of these three elements, they are all essential to planning, both at the level of whole school curriculum plans and at the level of specific schemes of work and topics. Part of the planning process should take account of the need to help learners understand their interrelationship.

The broad outline structure for every child's entitlement in environmental education is based on two broad areas which relate to the core and foundation subjects.

1 *Knowledge and understanding*
   (a) Knowledge about the environment at a variety of levels (ranging from local to global).
   (b) Knowledge and understanding of environmental issues at a variety of levels, (ranging from local to global).
   (c) Knowledge of alternative attitudes and approaches to environmental issues and the value systems underlying such attitudes and approaches.

2 *Skills*
   (a) Finding out about the environment either directly through the
       environment or by using secondary resources.
   (b) Communicating:
       (i) knowledge about the environment;
       (ii) both the pupil's own and alternative attitudes to environ-
            mental issues, to include justification for the attitudes or
            approaches advanced.
   (c) Participation:
       (i) as part of group decision-making;
       (ii) as part of making a personal response.

The development of skills is, of course, vital, not only to sound planning
for topics in environment education but also to take account of the
inclusion and progressive development of cross-curricular skills in the
curriculum as a whole.

A major argument for cross-curricular themes is that they provide a
medium through which children can use and develop knowledge, understanding and skills acquired in other subject areas. This cross-fertilisation
helps to show children the relevance and value of skills which have often
been acquired in separate discipline areas. As a cross-curricular theme,
environmental education allows children the opportunity to understand
the many and varied environmental issues that surround them, how
decisions are made about the environment and how people can have the
opportunity of participating in the decision-making process. Topics in
environmental education are thus a good opportunity for children to use
a whole range of skills in a way which is both relevant to their lives as well
as useful to their future as citizens.

Meticulous planning for such cross-curricular topics is crucial. A planning model will need to take account of the environmental elements
described (learning for, from and about the environment), as well as cross-
links with core and foundation subjects. Both of these components should
reflect the relevant range of knowledge, understandings and skills covered
in each, and a great deal of common ground should be demonstrated. This
model will no doubt sound very complex. A simpler analysis of the environmental topics, key issues and first hand experiences involved, knowledge
and understanding to be developed, is a good place to start. This information
can then be mapped on to the attainment targets and programmes of study
of core and foundation subjects in order to build up a more complex planning model. Precise learning objectives and attitudes that it is planned to
develop across the curriculum as a whole can then be identified.

As with all subject areas of the National Curriculum, planning for
cross-curricular themes cannot be separated from assessment procedures.

Furthermore, because of their cross-curricular nature, assessment of such themes will need to take account of the whole curriculum.

A point to bear in mind is that whilst the national framework for assessment will need to be considered as a baseline because a great deal of environmental learning will occur through teaching of core and foundation subjects, innovatory methods of environmental assessment will need to be developed by individual schools in relation to awareness, skills and the formation of values and attitudes. Individual pupil records and profiles will form a basis for this.

Records are, of course, an essential component of the assessment/evaluation task. Documentation may comprise a wide range of written material including pupil profile sheets, test results, notes or diaries of observations, samples of children's work and class records/summary of content records. As with all records, the prepared documents will serve a variety of purposes, and are of particular importance when developing cross-curricular work as they:

• will inform planning for the permeation of environmental education (or any other theme) across the statutory subjects;
• will record achievement of individual learners and help with an understanding of development of the relevant knowledge, skills and attitudes across the curriculum;
• will help with an understanding of how learners are appreciating the interrelationship that exists amongst tasks about the environment, for the environment and in/from the environment.

Further discussion on record keeping and examples of 'tried and tested' tables to record skill development in environmental education can be found in Neal and Palmer (1990).

No individual topics or schemes for environment education will be planned and implemented successfully unless it is within the context of a whole school policy and framework for this area. Arrangements for cross-curricular issues cannot be left to chance or individual enthusiasms. Whole school planning will ensure consistency, coverage and progression. Initial staff discussion on the formulation of a school policy will no doubt need to focus on such matters as

• What are our present arrangements?
• How are we to set environmental education in the context of the framework for the whole curriculum?
• What about approaches to teaching and learning – consistency and progression of topics etc.?
• How will time be organised and prioritised?
• What about resources/storage and distribution of materials?
• How will we ensure environmental curriculum continuity and coverage?

- What forms will assessment and record-keeping take?
- How will the school policy and individual topics be monitored and evaluated?
- How do we achieve a balance between flexibility/individual pupil interest and choice and the time constraints of core curriculum areas?

A policy document deriving from such discussions will usefully contain eight sections. As much or as little as the school requires may be included under the following headings, conditioned by local choice, and, not least, by the existing curriculum statements for the school.

- Aims
- Objectives
- Methods and timing
- Content (knowledge, understanding, skills, concepts, attitudes)
- Resources and organisation of resources
- Assessment, record keeping and evaluation
- The school itself as an environmental stimulus
- Other matters (e.g. links with community, fieldwork, policy for school grounds development and maintenance)

(Neal and Palmer 1990)

In conclusion, a return to a central theme of this book. Many find it difficult to envisage how teachers can justify delivery of the National Curriculum other than in terms of it being instrumental for achieving targets of attainment. A concern expressed by many is that early years topic work must necessarily give way, to some extent at least, to the imposition of subject boundaries and prescribed schemes of work. Yet legislation allows for some freedom of interpretation, certainly for the implementation of teaching and learning strategies considered appropriate by an individual teacher, and above all, for the continuation and development of the existing good practice which characterises learning in so many early years classrooms. Central to the National Curriculum documentation is the notion that a broad, balanced and meaningful education in the core and foundation subjects is a basic entitlement of all children. The concrete example outlined in the case study illustrates that this may be achieved through an integrated, topic-based approach to learning, based on a cross-curricular theme.

In Waverley Cross School environmental education is taking place within the children's familiar surroundings. The knowledge, understanding and processes of other areas such as science and geography are being developed in the context of the pupil's individual potential and natural curiosity. The approach to organisation is through a topic which clearly has cross-curricular issues as the central core. It is apparent that other areas of the curriculum arise from and underpin this core.

Cross-curricular skills such as detailed observation, investigation and problem-solving are essential to the tasks being undertaken. The learners readily demonstrate a capacity to make connections, to discover and to test their own ideas, arguments and discoveries. The approach builds upon the natural experiences which young children automatically bring from the world around them to each learning situation. Through these experiences the children continually develop ideas which enable them to make increasing sense of their environment and of the interrelationships that exist among things and happenings within it. It is intended that pupils' knowledge and understanding and ability for problem-solving will progressively increase as new experiences with objects and events are encountered, and as skills of investigation and exploration are developed.

The approach is successful in that it powerfully motivates those involved and addresses the statutory content of National Curriculum documentation. Furthermore, it demonstrates that the cross-curricular theme of environmental education can be a highly successful starting point or unifying element in National Curriculum delivery.

There can be no 'right or wrong' way to approach the teaching and learning of cross-curricular issues, yet coherence to the overall curriculum jigsaw would seem essential if progress is to be made in any of its constituent parts. There can be little doubt that a well-planned topic work approach is the most appropriate way of ensuring the inclusion of cross-curricular elements in the first three years in school.

Chapter 8

English and topic work

INTRODUCTION

Paradoxically, although English is one of the core subjects in the National Curriculum and pervades the whole of teaching, it tends to receive less attention than other subjects when topic work is being discussed. No one doubts the importance of English, so it might become almost taken for granted. This chapter is about the place of English in topic work and elsewhere in the infant curriculum. It may seem a pity to appear to narrow the horizons of the subject by using the word English instead of the broader term language. Use of the latter, amongst other advantages, encourages the consideration of all languages, acknowledging the cultural diversity of British society. It also illustrates the need for teachers to be conversant with language acquisition and the nature of language. However, while using the term English and considering how this may be taught within the framework of English 5–16 (DES 1990a) we have these issues in mind. We do not doubt that teachers will incorporate the contributions of all children and honour bilingualism and mother tongues whatever they are. Learning how to develop what they already know about speaking, listening, reading and writing is the entitlement of all our children. This is the case whether or not their first language is English. What all children know about language is the foundation on which teachers build a better understanding of English. All our children can be empowered to use English, to know about its forms, its literature and its diversity. To be able to do this does not in any way denigrate the language of their homes, be this Urdu or their regional dialect of English (or both!). Of course, depth of understanding of diversity may not be possible in infant classrooms and is not required by the National Curriculum until level 5. Nevertheless, a start is made by teachers' acceptance of the language found in children's homes which is brought to school.

Teachers do not automatically correct spoken regional deviations from generally accepted forms, as they are aware that these are neither slipshod nor lazy but part of the grammar of the district. Nor do they object to vocabulary which is part of that tradition. The word 'belly' is normal speech in the home city of one of the writers. It was good enough for Shakespeare. . . . More seriously, schools and teachers as part of their English policy are aware of and sensitive to children's huge achievements in language acquisition outside school and the need to see parents as partners in further developments.

Until very recently, it was not uncommon to hear the comment that English, in all its forms, has been neglected since the advent of the National Curriculum. The press for coverage of all the other subjects is blamed. It is also possible that because teaching takes place using the English language in talking, reading and writing, that the programmes of study in English (DES 1990a) will be met automatically and incidentally. Indeed much of it will be met through children's implicit knowledge. However, this may not always be the case. Progress in English has to be planned, and progress in all subjects is dependent to some extent on progress in English. The ability of children to talk with each other and their teachers about their work is crucial to their understanding of all subjects. Writing is one of the ways in which thinking is clarified and extended. 'Writing is, par excellence, the activity in which we consciously wrestle with thoughts and words in order to discover what we mean' (Wells 1986). Reading is an activity that can take children out of the here and now, broaden their experience as almost no other medium can, and introduce them to abstract concepts.

Apart from being an essential element in all learning, English is also a subject in its own right. Learning about the language itself, its creative, expressive and instrumental functions, needs a broad base. It should not be explored invariably as a vehicle in support of other subjects. There is an excellent range of literature available to children from British and other authors nowadays and children can be given the chance to enjoy this to the full. In order to learn about the language and its literature, which are inextricably intertwined at this age, children need a curriculum which is broad, but stresses the importance of English. Suggestions are made in this chapter about this curriculum. It is argued that there is a place for activities specific to English. In addition, English must be a support to all topics but whether topics are broadly based or subject focused, objectives specific to the English curriculum can be identified. Finally, and particularly about literature, topics focused on English can be a valuable part of the curriculum. These dimensions will be discussed in detail. The English components of two topics will be outlined: one is focused on the subject of history and one is broadly based. A further topic will be described which has English as the main focus.

An examination of the programmes of study for each aspect of English at Key Stage 1 (DES 1990a) and teachers' knowledge of how children's learning develops over time, suggests that their attainment levels will differ a great deal, not only across the whole programme of study but between each attainment target. For each topic, therefore, a suitable age will be suggested, in the knowledge that whether or not it is appropriate will depend on individual classes and individual children. It would also become tedious and unnecessarily repetitive to state, for each topic, what has been written before. Therefore, before any of the topics are outlined, English features which appear frequently in all of them will be identified. This general section will include reference to work which may be needed outside of topics and will occasionally step outside the requirements of the National Curriculum where this seems necessary. Comments which appear within each topic will be restricted as far as possible to more specific points. In identifying common features it will be necessary to quote statements of attainment. We apologise for including material so familiar to teachers but hope that this is accepted for ease of reference.

SOME GENERAL COMMENTS ON THE ENGLISH CURRICULUM AND TOPIC WORK

The reading environment

Central to the reading environment that teachers establish in their classrooms are the stories, poems and all the reading material to which children are introduced. Naturally, the programmes of study for English abound with references to the importance of this material: 'Pupils should encounter an environment where they are surrounded by books and other reading material presented in an attractive way' (DES 1990a). Children should not only 'encounter the environment' but more explicitly be read to and read constantly. To start with we concentrate on stories and poems which are read to children.

> [L]istening to stories and discussing them with adults in ways that lead children to reflect upon their own experience and encourage them to explore, through their imagination, the world created through the language of the text . . . are probably the experiences that help most young children to discover and begin to take control of what Sapir called 'the dynamo of language'.
>
> (Wells 1986)

The statements of attainment in the National Curriculum related to stories and poems which are read to children are:

AT1 level 1b listen attentively and respond to stories and poems
AT1 level 2c listen attentively to stories and poems and talk about them
AT2 level 1d talk in simple terms about the content of stories . . .
AT2 level 2d describe what happened in a story and predict what may happen next

AT2 level 2e listen and respond to stories and poems . . . read aloud expressing opinions informed by what has been read
AT2 level 3c listen attentively to stories, talk about setting, story line, characters and recall significant details
AT2 level 3 demonstrate in talking about stories that they are beginning to use inference, deduction and previous reading experience to find and appreciate meanings beyond the literal.

(DES 1990a)

It is clear that, if only to meet the attainment targets, reading to children is essential in the early years curriculum. Beyond that, the power of listening to stories and poems as models for writing, for the introduction of new experiences and concepts, for promoting thinking and participation and for the pleasure they give makes them an essential element in the curriculum.

Looking at the statements of attainment reinforces the point made above that the sorts of responses and understandings children bring to this activity will vary enormously and that teachers will need to read to classes and smaller groups from a wide range of books. Teachers do not select books simply at the children's level. By their skill in reading and talking with children they should enable them to get to grips with more complex ideas beyond this level. As far as topic work is concerned, there are many stories and poems which can be used, and in the history topic, the particular value of stories to help children understand other subjects will be discussed. What the teacher aims to achieve by reading or telling stories and poems, however, will always be similar, whether or not these aims are topic related. They include pleasure, excitement, satisfaction, participation, empathy and the experience of becoming 'hooked on books'. Exposure to stories and poems is too important to be limited by topic work. It is necessary to continue to read stories which are not related to topics as well as those which are. Sometimes it is hard to find good stories to fit a topic. Sometimes a teacher may be tempted to use a story which is less than excellent, just because it happens to fit the topic. However, there are so many exciting, well-written stories and poems which can be read with children, including those from many cultures, that it seems a waste to select the second rate to read to children. In short, if there isn't a good connected story, read something that isn't connected.

However, there is no intention to be elitist or to impose censorship in the reference to the 'second rate'. As Elaine Moss wrote

The artistically worthless book – hack written and poorly illustrated – may, if its emotional content is sound, hold a message of supreme significance for a particular child . . . . For a book by itself is nothing – a film shown in an empty cinema: one can only access its value by the light it brings to a child's eye.

(Moss 1977)

Nevertheless, time to read to and with children is limited and teachers want to introduce children to the best that is available. Teachers often find themselves in a dilemma when children ask them to read books, annuals, comics, etc. brought from home. These may not be the sort the teacher would have selected but the children must be encouraged and a compromise must be made. What is read to or by children in the classroom will include 'the best that is available' selected by the teacher, but it should also include books, annuals and comics chosen by the children. Whatever will encourage them to become readers should be used.

What comprises 'the best' is hard to define. Teachers should enjoy the stories and poems themselves, bearing in mind that some books intended for children appeal more to adults. The best fiction and poetry for children seem to be those written by authors who can get into the minds of children and who write directly for them. Good illustrations match the authors' intentions. Many authors and illustrators become popular because their books have a universal appeal which stands the test of time. Their books are believable even when the characters and events are impossible in reality. They take children from their own experience into a world illuminated by the author's imagination. They satisfy by expert plots and fascinate by their use of language. They involve children in sympathy, empathy, indignation and excitement and in many of the best books they make children laugh.

The attainment targets quoted above did not include those which refer to children learning to read and reading for themselves. Of course, reading to children is integral to these processes as it provides the models and discussions which children apply to their own reading and to their own writing. Children who can do so, will read stories, poems and other material provided during a topic, which are related to it. No one is likely to dispute, however, that children will still be learning to read elsewhere with the help of teachers, other adults or other children; whether they are doing so with the aid of a reading scheme or from other books or both. The range of material to read will be extended by topic work but cannot replace that which teachers have identified as most suitable to help children become readers. Whatever method is chosen to teach reading there will always be substantial elements of choice available to children. We know children who have made the breakthrough to reading ('this means something to me') through such diverse materials as comics, annuals and articles on BMX bikes.

Reading for information

Reading to children and by children to further knowledge and obtain information is not confined to non-fiction. All the books through which children learn to read including those read to them, will extend their knowledge, but in this section we are concerned specifically with information books which are non-fiction. The most relevant statements of attainment are:

> AT2 level 1d talk in simple terms about the content of stories or information in non-fiction books
> AT2 level 2e listen and respond to stories, poems and other material read aloud expressing opinions informed by what has been read
> AT2 level 2f read a range of material with some independence, fluency, accuracy and understanding
> AT2 level 3 devise a clear set of questions that will enable them to select and use appropriate information sources and reference books from the class and school libraries.
>
> (DES 1990a)

If there is a wide range of non-fiction books of an attractive nature, including good encyclopaedias, available in the class, children should be encouraged to select their chosen reading from these as well as from fiction. Apart from this, however, information books are used in context for specific purposes and this will often be in topics. There seems little to recommend about text books which flit around various subjects requiring children to answer questions about de-contextualised passages of text containing snippets of information.

For learning across the curriculum, well-written information books related to each subject are required. Unfortunately, to provide even a minimal supply of such books and additional written material is very expensive and in many areas (but not all) suitable information books at Key Stage 1 are in short supply although the situation is improving. Books can of course, be borrowed from LEA sources and local libraries and many museums lend out packs which include written material, for example, facsimile period newspapers. Because teachers will have to use what they can get hold of and because – unlike good stories and poems – information books can become dated, none are named in support of the topics which follow. If different subjects and/or parts of subjects had been selected for these topics some information books might have been mentioned. There are quantities of information books available about space, for example, and many on geography and the environment. If a period of history had been selected and not 'Toys and games' (the Victorians, for example), much more material would have been available. Frequently, however, a teacher will find that as in the case of the topic called 'Toys and games', she or he will need a number of wide ranging books, where the information required is scattered and hard for children to extract. Instead of naming information books in the topics, therefore, a number of ideas are given below about the selection and use of information books, taking into account the constraints of expense and availability.

Some books and other material, such as leaflets published by museums and packs obtainable from industry, are useful to teachers. Other sources for such material include publications by such bodies as the National Trust and the Royal Society for the Protection of Birds. Browsing amongst remaindered books and in book sales is often rewarded inexpensively. No teacher can be a fund of information across all the subjects in the curriculum. Very often she or he will have to read up on a subject. The books and materials collected and used for this purpose will enable the teacher to convey accurate information to children (and must therefore be accurate). Conveying information to children does not mean that a teacher cannot, at times, share the fact that she or he is also a learner of an unfamiliar subject. However, schools need to build up gradually a collection of books for teachers. (The need for the collection of teaching packs which includes books was stressed in the chapter on history and this advice is relevant to most if not all the subjects in the curriculum.) Books and other written material collected for use by teachers will often be too difficult for children although, if the books are well illustrated and captioned, some use of them may be made by the class. Teachers will need to be familiar with such adult books so they can help children if they want to make use of them.

Books which children can begin to use themselves need careful selection. In the first place they need to be checked, as far as possible, for accuracy. Some surprising howlers can be found in poor texts.

It can be useful, however, to get children to criticise inaccurate information or uninteresting texts. They can begin to challenge sources and see that what is written in a book (or a newspaper) is not necessarily the whole truth. In our experience, the best information books for children have a named author and illustrator and are not compiled (apparently) by an anonymous committee. The text should be clear and readable at suitable levels and the illustrations should be attractive and captioned, where appropriate. Some books waver confusingly between narrative and information and back again. These are probably best avoided. It is important to check that any book chosen for purchase has a list of contents, an index and, if possible, a glossary. A glossary often identifies key words and concepts the children need to grasp (and be able to spell on occasion). Some more recent books also include a bibliography which can be used to point out to children the fact that any one book is necessarily limited and that there is a need to look further. Older books often omit these features. No school can afford to discard all its old books but those which are retained should be selected on grounds of merit. Poor models include books which give snatches of information across a content which is too wide and a theme which is very loosely connected. Some are out of date – 'One day man may land on the moon' – and some contain inaccurate information. Some of these books may provide pictures and bits of text which can be cut up as a resource or they may be used to enable children to be critical as suggested above.

Introducing children to the use of information books starts well before level 3. Even before children can read they will witness that teachers use books for information and the children themselves can often get information from pictures. At all levels teachers will read to children from suitable information books. The ways in which language is structured in information books provides further models for children's writing. Children should be encouraged to browse through information books which have been collected for a topic. However, they should also be shown, from the outset, that although information can be gathered from reading a whole book this is different from going to books with specific questions to be answered in mind. A request to children: 'What can you find out about garden birds from these books?' leads to chunk copying. 'What questions can you ask about a robin?' leads to careful search and early use of contents and indices.

As has been indicated, in some areas of the curriculum information books which are suitable for young children are few on the ground. Here it is sensible for children to write their own information books. Even if books are available, this activity provides a different genre for writing. Children often write their own story books for others to read. This activity is just as valuable if they write non-fiction. Children are pleased to read the books they write and that others have written, individually or in a group. In writing information books, children will also become familiar with the use of contents pages, indices, glossaries and even bibliographies often more productively than when they see these items in commercial publications. Writing information books also gives purpose to the knowledge they have gleaned. It is common for classes to produce 'Our book about . . .'. We extend this idea to suggest that the books the children produce have the characteristics of good information books that have been identified above. This suggestion is recorded in the section on reading rather than writing but, of course, whatever writing children do is for reading: by themselves, by teachers and by other children and whenever possible, a wider audience.

Writing across the curriculum

'Pupils should have frequent opportunities to write in different contexts and for a variety of purposes and audiences including themselves' (DES 1990a). Topic work provides many reasons for writing in many different genres. The statements of attainment for attainment target 3, Writing (DES 1990a) specify progress from 'using pictures, symbols or isolated words and phrases to communicate meaning' (AT 3 level 1) to 'independent writing using complex sentences, simple punctuation, a wider range of connectives than "and" and "then" and revision and redrafting of texts' (level 3). Along the way, chronological and non-chronological writing are exemplified as:

Chronological accounts: 'an account of a family occasion, a practical task in mathematics or an adventure story' (Level 2b)

'A story with an opening which suggests when or where the action takes place and which involves more than one character' (Level 2c)

Use of 'but, when, after, so because' (Level 3b)

'Stories which include a description of setting and the feeling of characters' (Level 3c)

Nonchronological writing: 'lists, captions, invitations, greeting cards, notices, posters, etc.' (Level 2d)

Plans and diagrams, descriptions of a person or place or notes for an activity or design (Level 3d)

(DES 1990a)

The nonstatutory examples have been given here rather than detailing the statements of attainment because the latter refer only to either chronological writing (including story) or non-chronological writing. They also make an abrupt transition from early mark making and single words to more accepted conventional writing. The development of writing *per se* is not our major concern and readers are referred to other sources of information such as Kress (1982) and Nicholls *et al.* (1989). In respect of the reference to chronological and non-chronological writing, the statements of attainment are also not very helpful unless the range of writing to which these terms could refer is considered. This range of writing is what has been referred to above as genre, and children come to realise that there are distinctions, for example, between story and between other ways of writing (Nicholls *et al.* 1989). It is the content of the different genres of writing that we wish to consider in relation to topic work and not the teaching of spelling, handwriting and presentation. These skills are important and their development is taught and learned in any writing that children do, but our focus is content, context and purposes for writing and where these are found in topics. On the whole, topics provide purposes for writing in any of the genres for which examples are given in the attainment targets and for many others such as instructions, information for others, collections of favourite poems, and more complex symbols such as items on a map etc.

It may or may not be appropriate for children to write in a story format in some topics. Writing stories is the first, most natural and important genre of writing that children do. However, there is a distinction between story in the sense being addressed as opposed to all narrative. For example 'The story of electricity' is not a 'story' if the term is defined as a fictional artform such as a novel or a fairy story. Nevertheless, 'storying' in a more general sense appears to be a fundamental human activity and a way in which we learn and make sense of the world. 'Constructing stories in the mind . . . is one of the most fundamental means of making meaning: as such it is an activity that pervades all aspects of learning' (Wells 1986).

As far as writing is concerned, children will 'story' about anything they learn. The point is not that they should be discouraged from doing so but that they should begin to understand story as a fictional and specific form, and the differences between it and other sorts of writing. To this end perhaps it is not sensible to put all forms of writing in 'your story book'. If a teacher wishes at an appropriate point to discuss, for example, how to improve the structure of a story, the children need to know what sort of writing she is talking about. There will be times when a story is called for in topics, but the other forms of writing to which children can be introduced may also arise. These would include letters, lists, descriptions, recipes, instructions, reports of experiments and the information books referred to above. In any event, however, it seems necessary that children should be encouraged to write, whether in stories or other formats out-side of topics, particularly when they themselves choose to do so. A topic may provide part of such choice, for example, in the post office, the clinic, or the travel agent's engendered by a topic. Nevertheless good practice such as the private books children elect to write in, diaries and writing bays might continue to be used.

Children need to write for themselves. Poetry especially may need to be a personal and private experience. They also need to develop a further sense of audience other than the teacher. Their friends provide one of the first audiences. As well as notices, labels, writing on display and books for the class to read they should be encouraged to share their texts with neighbouring children, especially during the process. (This would include writing done with a partner or a group.) Reading complete or incomplete writing to peers provides a means for self-correction and a sense of the reader's needs which may be more useful than a teacher's response (Nicholls *et al.* 1989). Extending the sense of audience obviously requires further audiences. In the topics which follow letters are often used.

Topics can provide many other genres of writing with a specific audience in mind other than that immediately to hand. These might include:

- posters, notices and newspapers for other classes, the junior school and parents;
- guidebooks and catalogues for all visitors (the local tourist office might like copies of guides to the environment as would the local library);
- book reviews for other classes and the local library;
- information books and stories for other classes in the school or for other schools;

- copies of assembled children's work for museums and other places visited;
- books as presents for teachers and other staff who are leaving;
- guides to the school itself (its staff, layout, history, procedures, rules, according to which has been studied) to be given to parents, visitors and governors.

Having stressed the importance of writing it must be said that sometimes children may be asked to 'write about it' too often. There are other ways of recording and communicating: drawing, painting, modelling, data display or just talking about an experience.

Writing is often a task which is set without differentiation for a whole class, in the expectation that the outcomes will be at various levels. Sometimes this is appropriate, but in the topics which follow different levels of tasks have been indicated in places. It is also sometimes necessary for the teacher to work with children who are writing more often than is common practice in, say, mathematics. Children working and collaborating with the teacher as well as other children enables progress to be made at any level (Nicholls *et al.* 1989).

Discussions and conversations between the teacher and children and between children

Through the Programmes of Study pupils should encounter a range of situations, audiences and activities which are designed to develop their competence in speaking and listening, irrespective of their initial competence or home language.

(DES 1990a)

The topics to be described, like all activities in the infant classroom, have oral language as a central component. Some children are more reluctant than others to talk, at least to teachers, in school, although it is often salutary to hear them in the playground or to encounter them outside school in the supermarket, for example. However, their confidence and ability to articulate what they know will grow. In the meantime, teachers are aware that 'show me' rather than 'tell me' is sensible. Nevertheless, it should be remembered that the achievement of the following attainment targets is an aim. (Those that have been cited already for story are omitted.)

AT1

Level 1a	participate as speakers and listeners in group activities including imaginative play
Level 1c	respond appropriately to simple instructions given by the teacher

Level 2a	participate as speaker and listeners in a group engaged on a given task
Level 2b	describe an event, real or imagined to the teacher or another pupil
Level 2d	talk with the teacher, listen and answer questions
Level 2e	respond appropriately to a range of more complex instructions given by a teacher and give simple instructions
Level 3a	relate real or imagined events in a connected sequence
Level 3b	convey accurately a simple message
Level 3c	talk with an increased span of concentration to other children and adults, asking and responding to questions and commenting on what has been said
Level 3d	give and receive and follow accurately precise instructions.

(DES 1990a)

There seems little in these attainment targets that cannot be incorporated into topics. Teachers have to decide about such matters as group size when they are talking with children. It is clear that the teacher's task is not easy simply because of the problems of engaging thirty or so children in conversation. The indirect and polite forms of command normally used in school have not been found to cause any difficulties (Wells 1986). Conversations are another matter. In chapter 1 a conversation between a parent and a child was described in which the child gained some insights into a complex concept, assisted by talking with an interested and supportive adult. These sorts of interactions are invaluable to learning in general and to speaking and listening in particular. Teachers generally try to make space for them in the odd moments they can seize and they have been urged by Wells (ibid.), for example, to arrange conversation in smaller groups than the class. It has been suggested that another way to make space for more group and individual conversations is for teachers to identify more activities in which they teach the whole class (Alexander *et al.* 1992). Because it is not possible to have a discussion with thirty or so participants, in many class sessions the teacher might deploy his or her skills at exposition, showing and telling and giving examples but not expecting the sort of participation that could really be called a discussion. (This does not apply to story sessions which can enable class participation, although story with a small group is very beneficial.) So-called class discussions have been found to have 'strained quality' (Desforges and Cockburn 1987) and could be reduced in quantity, using the time saved for better teaching in groups and for individual interactions.

Of course, there is a place for introducing new programmes to a class and in the topics these introductions have been specified. One should always be aware, however, that there will be some children for whom it would be necessary to go over things again after any class session. In the topics outlined there will also be many activities which call for children to talk to each other as well as to the teacher.

Outside of topics there may be a need for children to explore the sounds and meanings of their language. For example, in a topic on sound, children might play around with onomatopoeic words like 'smash' and 'crash' or invent their own words. But if no topic was available it might still be necessary to do something like this. Another example is collections of words that sound the same but are spelled differently such as 'bare' and 'bear'. Parents may like to contribute to these but of course regional pronunciation will produce variations. This, of course, is a good time to talk about such differences in an unthreatening way. These are just two examples. There are many other ways of playing with words and meanings which is as important to English as playing with numbers is to mathematics.

Role play and drama

Imaginative play, role play and drama are essential components of the curriculum. The last topic to be described lends itself to a full development of this area but it can arise in any topic. Any play-related activity – a space capsule, a shop, a travel agent, a cafe, a model of the local streets – has role play, speaking and listening as its purposes. These activities can be extended by using puppets and then into drama in the classroom or in the hall.

Assessment

Assessment in English is very much an ongoing process. That is, it is unlike a summative assessment of a body of knowledge which might follow teaching which had limited and specific objectives. Reading is assessed every time a teacher reads with a child. Speaking and listening require that teachers are alert to children's uses of spoken English and keep a diary of their achievements and problems. A teacher might decide to use a particular writing task for specific assessment. However, this would augment the file of dated written work which accumulates over time, presenting a picture of progress. Of course, all these observations and pieces of evidence would be used to plan further work for each child, but progress in English varies enormously with context and opportunity and seems to progress and regress in those contexts. For example, if the composition of a story takes over, spelling and presentation can become very erratic (Nicholls *et al.* 1989). Assessment in English is necessarily an area in which progress must be ascertained by continuous tentative judgements made over time.

The divisions which have been made above between various facets of learning about English are frequently artificial. It is not really possible to separate reading from writing or indeed from talking. Nevertheless they draw attention to the care that is needed in thinking about what the English component of the curriculum consists of within and outside of topics. This chapter will conclude with descriptions of the three topics that have been promised.

THREE TOPICS AND THEIR ENGLISH COMPONENTS

Each of the topics has been used in classrooms in some form or other, none very different from what is described. They have had to be updated where necessary to meet the requirements of the National Curriculum. A different format will be used to describe each topic in order to focus on different facets of planning. The first topic is focused on another subject, in this case, history.

A history-focused topic – Toys and games

This topic is planned for children at the end of year 1. A project on toys and games has instant appeal to young children and relates directly to their own experience. Any historical topic which is not specific to an era or incident in history ('The 1940s', 'Captain Cook') requires decisions about how far back in the past it is sensible to go. Toys and games reach far back into history with evidence, for example, of Ancient Egyptians playing board games and playing with marbles. For this dip into the past the main thrust is within living memory, with a little on the Edwardian and Victorian eras depending on the material and evidence available. Elements beside history and English will be mentioned but only in passing. History is a subject which requires extensive use of the oral tradition, written evidence of all kinds and a disciplined use of the imagination, and as such is ideal to use in demonstrating the use of English in a topic on another subject.

Progress and development of the topic

This account enters the topic at a point following initial planning of content and purposes for learning and where the order in which activities are to be presented has been decided.

1 The teacher reads the story *Dogger* (Hughes 1977) with the class. Children are responsive to this story in which a small boy and his sister love soft toys. She collects them. He has one favourite called Dogger. Dogger gets lost but turns up at a fair on a jumble stall. Before the little boy can tell anyone, Dogger is sold to another child. However, the sister

has won a magnificent teddy in a raffle. She wants it but swaps it for Dogger because she loves her little brother. The story introduces the theme well because most children have a 'Dogger' of their own. It can also be used for moral and religious development.

After the story has been read and talked about children are asked to make a further response according to attainment level: orally, by drawing and painting or written descriptions or more than one of these. This response requires them to identify their favourite toys, especially those they had when they were very little.

Comment A historical objective is to begin to contrast now with the children's own past. In addition, one effect of reading stories with children at any time is that through their questions and the teacher's interpretations they begin to find out the difference between real (true) stories and ones which are imagined (history AT2 level 1, DES 1991c) This is not a process which could or should be hurried.

2 The teacher brings in an obviously old soft toy of his or her own or one belonging to a friend. Showing it to the children, they tell a story about it, bringing in the language of the past. They may also read *Old Bear* (Hissey 1991). There are several stories in this series where an old worn teddy bear is the main character and the others are soft toys. This is the stimulus for asking children if there are any old toys at home they can bring in, explaining why they are needed. As a class activity, a letter is composed to parents with teacher as scribe to ask for their help. It will need to explain, for example, that there will be a history project about old toys, that a toy museum will be set up, that great care will be taken of toys, that if possible parents should say how old the toys are, that it would be appreciated if grandparents could be asked, and so on. A list of categories can be appended, planned by a group: old toy cars, soft toys, mechanical toys, boxed toys, etc. Here it is useful to have some information books to give ideas for the list. This request should bring a response, but teachers will need a fallback collection of their own. While the toys come in, the original soft toy belonging to a teacher – let us call him Albert – can have letters written to him by the children asking him about his history. Of course, the teacher will have to reply for Albert.

Comment The collaborative letter to parents is introductory to that genre of non-chronological writing. In the letters to Albert the teacher can assess what children have remembered about that format and can begin to introduce some of the differences which appear in letters according to audience and purpose.

Stories – oral or written – are important to teaching the content of many subjects, especially history. For young children they are often more powerful and meaningful than information books. They contain 'the age old power of the story to teach as it entertains' (Little 1989). A well-written story involves its audience, who identify with its characters, its situations and its settings. Children are often more likely to remember the information painlessly acquired in a story than that from a text book. History is a very abstract subject and the abstractions it contains are more easily grasped in a story. For example, one concept is that different people have different points of view which have to be taken into account when weighing up evidence. There are several stories which can illuminate this idea. For example, related to toys there is *Satchelmouse and the Doll's House* (Barber and Munoz 1987). In this story the magic mouse enables the heroine to go into her Victorian doll's house. She had expected to be the daughter of the house but instead is the skivvy. The difference between the experiences which might be encountered by two children of the same age in the same house is made clear by the story. Not about toys, but on the same lines is *The True Story of the 3 Little Pigs by A. Wolf* (Scieszka 1989). Other stories which are set in the past, peopled by characters who lived then 'enable children to make that imaginative leap into the past which genuine understanding of history demands' (Little 1989).

3 The collection of toys when assembled requires discussion and decision making. How should they be sorted, labelled, displayed? Displays of various sorts can be made according to type of toy, materials with which toys are made, e.g. metal, cloth, wood, and, of course, some attempt can be made to put them in chronological order. Different groups of children may come up with different ideas. Some sorting can be recorded by data display but one of them should use a timeline. Observational drawings may be used either in the data displays or the timeline. Children should decide how to set out the display of the actual toys and label them for the museum. This can be followed by making catalogues. It is expected that the museum will have visitors and the catalogues must consider that audience.

Comment Data display and sorting reinforce mathematical skills. Putting items in chronological order will be hard, but a best guess is not inappropriate to history. The timeline is a basic historical tool. Labelling and numbering items in the museum and perhaps giving it a name provides for different sorts of non-chronological writing. The labels enable children to contribute at various levels from using single words to more elaborate descriptions; 'The teddy bear my mum had when she was a little girl.' 'This car was new in 1970.' Catalogues will need titles, a list of contents and descriptions and drawings of each item. This work can be divided up to match the way the museum has been set out and to avoid any group having to do too much writing.

4 At this point a visit can be arranged from a parent or grandparent or if possible one of each generation. They will be asked to talk about the games they played when they were young and the toys they had. An older person may remember that he or she normally had only an orange and one present

in the Christmas stocking. To introduce the next phase they or teachers can talk about the games that were used in the playground when they were young such as the seasonal round of hoops and marbles, or later the hula-hoop era. Children will need to decide what questions to ask the visitors and the teacher. If the visitors do not do so the teacher can talk about playground games, skipping rhymes and dips.

Comment Oral evidence is essential to the study of history and, of course, these are examples of people 'storying' about their experiences. From these stories of experience there may be a further opportunity to contrast the evidence from different accounts. For English, the children will be listening to and talking with adults other than the teacher. Deciding on the questions to be asked provides for group discussion, another form of writing and an introduction to the sorts of skills needed to interrogate not only people but written material.

5 At this point a visit to a toy museum or part of a museum which contains toys would be an exciting experience. Many museums will set up sessions where children can handle objects under supervision.

Comment Such a visit would, of course, need preparation through talk and could be followed by some written work. The latter could take two main forms. One might be a chronological account of the visit and one descriptive writing about selected toys. These two are separated because children tend to focus on an outing as an outing – the bus trip is more important than teachers' notions about the other learning experiences. Children want to write about what is important to them and there is every reason why they should do so. Then they can focus on the historical element and use the non-chronological descriptive form of writing. Too many letters might get tedious. The museum should be thanked but perhaps a high attaining group could tackle this task. In short, the visit would provide for a wide range of English tasks.

6 Whether or not a visit can be arranged, a teacher can use the toys collected and introduce facsimile toys available from all museums and many craft shops to take the project further back into time. Facsimile toys include whips and tops, hoops, marbles, cotton reel knitting, spinning disks (a button on string works just as well), balls and cups, wooden acrobats, diabolo, skipping ropes, five stones and many others used during and since Victorian times. If teachers know cat's cradle they can show it to the children. Children can make many of these toys themselves for technology and design. The predominance of wood in these facsimiles can be contrasted with modern plastic, as can the metal used for toy cars. What has changed? What remains the same? Additional work can be done to the catalogues indicating that much work needs to be done before a product is finished.

7 As a second phase (if required), children can be reminded that some toys are for outside use and some indoors, and the former can be extended by the introduction of neglected playground games, skipping rhymes and dips (e.g. one potato, two potato . . .). Parents, other adults in the school and books can be consulted for the collection. Most adults remember some games and some have survived: What's the time Mr Wolf?, Farmer, farmer may I cross your golden river?, various forms of skipping rhymes are legion, as are dips. Children can try out games, learn the skipping rhymes and invent new dips. They can also draw diagrams or write instructions for other classes on how to play the games. On one occasion when this topic was taught it culminated in an assembly where children demonstrated the games to the school. One aim of that topic was to improve the quality of playground behaviour. Skipping ropes were issued at playtime and hopscotch pitches were painted in the yard.

Comment There is a wealth of material available from many sources on playground games and interesting regional variations abound. Some of the names of the games and toys mentioned above will be familiar to the reader and some will not, but it is not necessary to be prescriptive. More pertinent to English are the activities that can be done with any such collection such as learning by heart. Poetry will come, but easy repetitive rhymes make a good start. Reintroducing something different to do in the playground, where play can become too much of a rough and tumble (although there is a place for that), is a bonus strongly related to the English curriculum including part of its cultural heritage. This particular topic lends itself to several age levels with suitable adjustments and several formats.

The next topic has a slightly more limited application.

A broadly focused topic – the post office

To start this topic, a traditional first draft of a topic web is shown in Figure 8.1. It is deliberately broad. A first draft is just a way of making a start.

This topic is intended for year 2 of Key Stage 1. The draft is the sort from which teachers draw out schemes of work related to programmes of study and attainment targets in the National Curriculum. It doesn't work quite like that of course; teachers would know already, from their experience, that the topic would probably provide the objectives they need, but they work backwards and forwards between the possible content and the National Curriculum to refine their ideas. Following that, the various subjects would need elaboration before decisions about the starting points and progression of the topic were made. Here, a guide to such an elaboration is made about the English component. Naturally

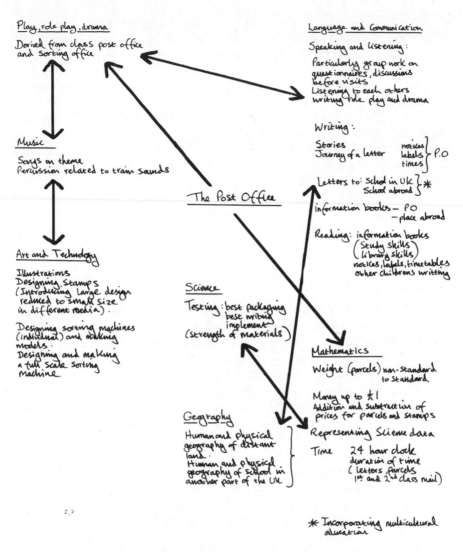

Play, role play, drama
Derived from class post office
and sorting office

Music
Songs on theme
Percussion related to train sounds

Art and Technology
Illustrations
Designing stamps
(Introducing large design
reduced to small size
in different media).

Designing sorting machines
(individual) and making
models.
Designing and making
a full scale sorting
machine

The Post Office

Science
Testing: best packaging
best writing
implement
(strength of materials)

Geography
Human and physical
geography of distant
land.
Human and physical
geography of school in
another part of the UK

Language and Communication
Speaking and listening:
Particularly group work on
questionnaires, discussions
before visits
Listening to each others
writing role play and drama

Writing:
Stories   notices
Journey of a letter   labels } P.O
                           times
Letters to: School in UK } *
            School abroad
information books — PO
             — place abroad
Reading: information books
         (study skills)
         (library skills)
         notices, labels, timetables
         other childrens writting

Mathematics
Weight (parcels) non-standard
                  to standard
Money up to £1
Addition and substraction of
prices for parcels and stamps
Representing Science data
Time   24 hour clock
        duration of time
        (letters, parcels
         1st and 2nd class mail)

* Incorporating multicultural
   education

Figure 8.1 The post office: a first draft of a topic web identifying content for year 2 infants

there would be overlap between subjects. For example, children would listen, question and contribute when teachers set up the conditions for the fair test of best ways to wrap a parcel and when they decide in groups how to represent that data. However, we shall point to some of the particular and important aspects of English which might be addressed in the topic.

Reading

A collection of stories, poems and information books is relatively easy to obtain for this topic – on the post office and on the country to be studied, for example – and often schools have such resources already. At this level – probably around level 2 and working towards level 3 for many children in a year 2 class – children can be introduced to or practise the skill of finding and selecting information books to use. They can investigate how the school library has been arranged for reference. (Probably they need to know the alphabet for this purpose.) They can also find, in advance, the questions they need to answer from the information books. They need information on the part of the United Kingdom and the distant land they intend to write to as well as on the postal system itself.

Other sorts of reading are found in the play post office set up in the topic. There is a need for labels and forms (to read as well as write), reading (and writing) the times and days of opening, and times and days of postal collections.

Writing

Letter writing is to the fore in this topic. Letters also featured in 'Toys and games' because they provide such a relevant purpose for writing – if you are going to get a reply. They are essential to this topic additionally because they provide information about how long letters take to get to their destinations by 1st class, 2nd class and air mail. If all else fails, children can correspond locally, but the advantages of writing to other parts of the United Kingdom and abroad, it is hoped, would outweigh the obvious chore of setting these situations up. Writing to another part of this country and abroad can meet geographical objectives. Writing to people in these places who have very different backgrounds and cultures from the children's own, provides the nearest thing to first hand experience that may be available. This is especially useful if the children in a school are all white or are all middle class or if the school is in an inner city or has a very rural setting. A school implementing a topic like this corresponded with children in the USA. The children wrote about their Christmas holidays and were surprised and interested when their pen friends were almost all Jewish and wrote about their own festivals in reply.

As we have noted, letters are written in various styles which change according to audience. (Contrast a job application with a letter to a close friend.) Letters to pen friends become more relaxed and there is no reason for correspondence, once begun, to cease with a topic. There might also be more formal letters, for example, to the local head post office requesting information and to the corner shop post office asking about a visit, or to the postman or postwoman thanking him or her for talking to the class.

Other types of writing might include a questionnaire for the postman, postwoman or the local post office. This sort of writing has a strong relationship to the questions children need to ask to get information from a book. Instructions might include how to wrap a parcel securely and how to address an envelope (with a postal code of course). Children can learn formats for scientific type reports. These might introduce the questions to be asked: What did we want to find out? What materials were used? What did we do? (method), What did we see? (observation), What did we find out? (conclusions), What else do we need to find out? (further research needed). As noted earlier, the play post office will need labels, forms, cheque books and notices to write and to read.

Speaking and listening

This aspect has been dealt with in the general section. However, it will be noticed that many opportunities for group work and collaborative decision making arise in this topic. These might include collaborative writing, of letters, for example, which promotes not only the writing, but speaking and listening with peers. The play post office is an example of the provision in a topic, for role play, which the teacher can enhance by sensitive intervention to assist in the elaboration of the imaginative play. Sometimes, teachers themselves will be in role.

The final topic to be outlined has English at its heart because it is focused on stories. It might well be a useful run up to a book week. These events are deservedly popular in schools as they indicate the value put on books. Often they include a visit from an author, an illustrator or story teller. This account is aimed at children around level 2, perhaps year 1 or 2 classes, but is adaptable to any age range.

A topic focused on English – Marvellous magical stories

This topic is also in the form of a draft which would be revised and refined in the light of further consideration. However, in this case it departs from the topic web and gives a different format for initial planning.

Aims

To spend about three weeks concentrating on different sorts of fiction to widen children's experience, to introduce specific issues such as gender and race and to attempt to enable as many children as possible to see that reading fiction is for them. To apply these aims to children's writing and oral language by the connections that will be made between the provision of stories and the children's writing and oral progress.

Objectives

(Most of these are derived from level 2 in English 5–16 (DES 1990a) but have been extended and amalgamated as necessary.)

- To read frequently to children in order to give them pleasure and interest.
- To enable them, in the context of the stories read, to listen and respond, to comment, to criticize, to contribute, to ask questions and to express opinions.
- To provide a wide range of fresh fiction for children to read for themselves, including the stories being read to them, at various levels of difficulty, to promote independent reading and enhance fluency and understanding.
- To ensure that children are given time to read, to encourage them to take books home and to provide reading conferences to help with choice, selectivity and discrimination.
- To incorporate the composition of oral story telling to reinforce notions about plot, character and structure.
- To encourage children to write their own stories linked to the weekly themes for specific audiences including themselves.
- To discuss the format of a story and what makes it interesting.
- To use role play and puppetry derived from the themes.

More objectives could have been specified but these may suffice as starting points.

Content

Over the three-week period a different theme in fiction is used each week and related to the aims and objectives specified above. In each week teachers read stories related to a theme, preferably more than once daily. They may decide that although story time makes a nice ending to the day, other times may be more productive. They may also introduce, if it is not normal practice, a time in the day when everyone reads. Sustained *silent* reading, particularly on introduction, may not be as important as children sharing books quietly. What is important is that everyone reads. Teachers also provide as many books as they can, related to the theme for the children to read or look at. They may also set up a library or play bookshop for role play and writing. A library can really lend books out and need not be restricted to the weekly theme. It can be embellished with pictures from favourite books, posters, and book reviews written by children. They will need to devise a recording system for lending books and a rota for staffing.

During each week children will be encouraged to write their own stories especially those stimulated by the theme. These can take various forms according to level of attainment. Zig-zag books (folded thin card with pictures at the top and text below) assist in structuring. The most able children may be introduced to rough planning notes. Books produced can add to the library stock, especially if printed up on a word processor, but all should have an author, an illustrator and a publisher (Class 5?). The class writing bay could be labelled 'author's corner do not disturb!'.

In addition, a suitable part of any of the weekly themes may be selected for drama or role play. Puppets may be useful to enable shyer children to join in. A further ongoing practice might be for teachers to demonstrate orally how to start a story and where to stop at an exciting point and have the children join in, either as a class or smaller group activity.

The theme for the first week is traditional fairy stories. Teachers may tell or read these and encourage children to tell, orally, those that they may remember. Fairy stories are by no means 'babyish'. There are many beautifully written picture books which are quite complicated, for example, *Melisande* (Nesbit 1989). *The Old Nursery Stories* (Nesbit 1981) is another good choice. It is also the case, as Kieran Egan points out, that fairy stories contain powerful 'binary opposites' (Egan 1985) such as power and powerlessness, rich and poor, good and evil, merchant and pauper, truth and lies (consider Dick Whittington for some of these). These are concepts which children are introduced to very early, and we might consider they would not be able to cope with them in any other medium.

This theme is particularly appropriate to children writing and illustrating books for younger children to read. Furthermore, as most fairy stories are firmly set in the past, they include a historical dimension using language such as 'a long time ago' and contribute, as most stories do to answering the question 'When am I?' Traditional tales should include stories from other cultures.

In the second week the question moves to 'Where am I?' because the stories are from round the world. There are many lovely story books containing geographical concepts so only *Stories Round the World* (The Federation of Children's Book Groups 1990) will be mentioned. This theme is also an excellent one for the introduction of books from other cultures so that multi-cultural issues can be discussed.

The final theme is modern stories about fantasy and magic. This also provides an opportunity to introduce gender because there are many stories in this genre which feature heroines, for example, *The Paper Bag Princess* (Munsch 1991) and *Nina's Machines* (Firmin 1989). *The Shrinking of Treehorn* and *Treehorn's Treasure* (Parry Heide 1986, 1988) are also modern magic and appeal to children because the adults in the stories never seem to listen or notice what is going on.

Although some stories have been suggested in the above account, there are thousands of others, and of course the themes can be altered to serve the teacher's purposes. It could be argued that more time might be needed or that the themes jump about rather abruptly. These again are matters for individual decision. The point can be made, however, that teachers do and should read regularly to children but sometimes with only very general purposes in mind. What has been suggested is that purposes for reading might be made more specific, in a topic, over and above the constant objective of introducing children to the fascinating world of fiction.

CONCLUSION

In the introduction we suggested that English is in danger of becoming less central to the early years curriculum due to the press for coverage of other subjects. We hope that we have demonstrated that the central place of English in the curriculum will not disturb, indeed it will enhance, children's learning in all areas of the curriculum.

Notes

3 HISTORY AND TOPIC WORK

1 The authors are grateful to the Head Teacher and staff of Holland House First School, Sutton Coldfield, West Midlands, for permission to include details of the case study on 'Images of our school'. Further discussion on this is found in Neal, P.D. and Palmer, J.A. (1990) *Environmental Education In The Primary School*, Oxford, Blackwell.

4 SCIENCE AND TOPIC WORK

1 The planning and implementation of this topic was in line with the original National Curriculum Order before revision of attainment targets. This does not detract from its value in demonstrating how planning took place and how work was developed. In this context, it is the issues and principles which are relevant, rather than precise content. Ideas for activities are nevertheless transferable.
2 Planning refers to the original NC ATs, and this does not detract from the essence of the discussion and key points made in the chapter.
3 The authors are grateful to the Head Teacher and staff of Holland House First School, Sutton Coldfield, West Midlands, for permission to include details of the case study topic 'For lunch today'.

References

Alexander, R. (1984) *Primary Teaching*, Eastbourne: Holt Rinehart & Winston Ltd.

Alexander, R.J. (1992) *Policy and Practice in Primary Education*, London: Routledge.

Alexander, R., Rose, J. and Woodhead, C. (1992) Curriculum organisation and class-room practice in primary schools: A discussion paper, DES.

Ausubel, D.P. (1968) *Educational Psychology: A Cognitive View*, New York: Holt, Rinehart & Winston.

Bale, J. (1987) *Geography in the Primary School*, London: Routledge & Kegan Paul.

Barber, R. Antonia and Munoz, C. (1987) *Satchelmouse and the Doll's House*, London: Walker Books.

Bennett, N. and Desforges, C. (1988) 'Matching classroom tasks to students attain-ments', *The Elementary School Journal* 88 (3), 222–34.

Bennett, N., Desforges, C., Cockburn, A. and Wilkinson, B. (1984) *The Quality of Pupil Learning Experiences*, London: Lawrence Erlbaum Associates.

Blenkin, G.M. and Kelly, A.V. (eds) (1983) *The Primary Curriculum in Action: A Process Approach to Educational Practice*, London: Harper & Row.

Blenkin, G.M. and Kelly, A.V. (1987) *The Primary Curriculum: A Process Approach to Curriculum Planing*, London: Harper & Row.

Blyth, J. (1989) *History in Primary Schools*, Milton Keynes: Open University Press.

Blyth, W.A.L. (1984) *Development Experience and Curriculum in Primary Education*, London: Croom Helm.

Boardman, D. (1983) *Graphicacy and Geography Teaching*, London: Croom Helm.

Bond, M. (1976) *A Bear Called Paddington*, London: Collins Lions.

Brophy, J. (ed.) (1989) *Advances in Research on Teaching*, Vol. 1, London: JAI Press.

Catling, S. (1978) 'Cognitive mapping exercises as a primary geographical experi-ence', *Teaching Geography* 3, 120–3.

Catling, S. (1988) 'Using maps and aerial photographs', in Mills, D. (ed.), *Geographical Work in Primary and Middle Schools*, Sheffield: The Geographical Association.

Cockcroft, W.H. (1982) *Mathematics Counts*, London: HMSO.

DES (1978) *Primary Education in England*, London: HMSO.

DES (1979) *Mathematics 5–11 A Handbook of Suggestions*, London: HMSO.

DES (1988) *Curriculum Matters Series*, London: HMSO.

DES (1989a) *Aspects of Primary Education: The Teaching and Learning of History and Geography*, London: HMSO.

DES (1989b) *Aspects of Primary Education: The Teaching and Learning of Science*, London: HMSO.

DES (1989c) *The Curriculum from 5–16, Curriculum Matters 2* (2nd edition, incor-porating responses), London: HMSO.

DES (1990a) *English in the National Curriculum (No. 2)*, London: HMSO.
DES (1990b) *History for Ages 5–16*, Proposals of the Secretary of State for Education and Science, London: HMSO.
DES (1991a) *Mathematics in the National Curriculum*, London: HMSO.
DES (1991b) *Geography in the National Curriculum*, London: HMSO.
DES (1991c) *History in the National Curriculum*, London: HMSO.
DES (1991d) *Science in the National Curriculum*, London: HMSO.
Desforges, A. and Desforges, C. (1980) 'Number based strategies in sharing in young children', *Education Studies* 6 (2), 97–109.
Desforges, C.W. (1989) 'Understanding learning for teaching', *Westminster Studies in Education* 12.
Desforges, C.W. and Cockburn, A. (1987) *Understanding the Mathematics Teacher*, Lewes: The Falmer Press.
Doise, W. and Mugny, G. (1984) *The Social Development of the Intellect*, Oxford: Pergamon.
Donaldson, M. (1978) *Children's Minds*, London: Fontana.
Egan, Kieran (1985) *Teaching as Story Telling*, London and Ontario: The Althouse Press.
Eisner, E.W. (1979) *The Educational Imagination*, London: Macmillan.
The Federation of Children's Book Groups (1990) *Stories Round the World*, Sevenoaks: Hodder & Stoughton Children's Books.
Fennema, E., Carpenter, T.P. and Peterson, P.L. (1989) 'Learning mathematics with understanding: cognitively guided instruction', in Brophy, J. (ed.), *Advances in Research on Teaching*, vol. I, London: JAI Press.
Ferreiro, E. and Teberosky, A. (1982) *Literacy before Schooling*, Portsmouth: V.H. Heinemann.
Firmin, P. (1989) *Nina's Machines*, London: Armada Books.
Fyson, N. (ed.) *The Development Puzzle*, London: Hodder & Stoughton/CDWE.
Gelman, R. and Gallistell, C.R. (1978) *The Child's Understanding of Number*, Cambridge, Mass. and London: Harvard University Press.
Hissey, J. (1991) *Old Bear*, London: Random Century.
Hughes, M. (1986) *Children and Number: Difficulties in Learning Mathematics*, Oxford: Basil Blackwell.
Hughes, M. (1989) 'The child as learner: the contrasting views of developmental psychology and early education', in Desforges, C.W. (ed.), *Early Childhood Education*, BJEP Monograph Series, Edinburgh, Scotland: Academic Press.
Hughes, Shirley (1977) *Dogger*, London: Bodley Head.
ILEA (1981) *The Study of Places in the Primary School*, London: ILEA.
Kress, G. (1982) *Learning to Write*, London: Routledge & Kegan Paul.
Little, V. (1989) 'Imagination and history', in Campbell, J. and Little, V. (eds), *Humanities in the Primary School*, London: The Falmer Press.
Morrison, K. (1989) Assessment, environmental education and the National Curriculum, National Association for Environmental Education Conference Paper, Durham.
Morrison, K. and Ridley, K. (1988) *Curriculum Planning and the Primary School*, London: Paul Chapman.
Moss, E. (1977) 'What is a "good" book', in Meek, M., Warlow, A. and Barton, G. (eds), *The Cool Web*, London: The Bodley Head.
Munsch, R.N. (1991) *The Paper Bag Princess*, Leamington Spa: Scholastic Children's Books.
NCC (1990) *Curriculum Guidance Series:*
   1. A Framework for The Primary Curriculum
   2. A Curriculum for All – Special Needs in The National Curriculum

3. The Whole Curriculum
4. Education for Economic and Industrial Understanding
5. Health Education
6. Careers Education and Guidance
7. Environmental Education
8. Education for Citizenship.
London: National Curriculum Council.

NCC (1991a) *History, Non-Statutory Guidance*, London: National Curriculum Council.

NCC (1991b) *Geography, Non-Statutory Guidance*, London: National Curriculum Council.

Neal, P.D. and Palmer, J.A. (1990) *Environmental Education In The Primary School*, Oxford: Blackwell.

Nesbit, E. (1981) *The Old Nursery Stories*, London: Hodder & Stoughton (Knight Books).

Nesbit, E. (1989) *Melisande*, London: Walker Books.

Nicholls, J., Bauer, A., Pettitt, D., Redgewell, V. and Watson, G. (1989) *Beginning Writing*, Milton Keynes: Open University Press.

Oliver, D. (1975) 'Skill centred teaching: an alternative to integration', *Education* 3 (1), 3–13.

Parry Heide, Florence (1986) *Treehorn's Treasure*, London: Puffin Books.

Parry Heide, Florence (1988) *The Shrinking of Treehorn*, London: Puffin Books.

Piaget, J. and Inhelder, B. (1956) *The Child's Conception of Space*, London: Routledge & Kegan Paul.

Piaget, J., Inhelder, B. and Szeminska, A. (1960) *The Child's Conception of Geometry*, London: Routledge & Kegan Paul.

Scieszka, J. (1989) *The True Story of 3 Little Pigs by A. Wolf*, London: Puffin Books.

Skemp, R.R. (1989) *Mathematics in the Primary School*, London: Routledge.

Tizard, B. and Hughes, M. (1984) *Young Children Learning: Talking and Thinking at Home and at School*, London: Fontana.

Tizard, B., Blatchford, P., Burke, J., Farquhar, C. and Plewis, I. (1988) *Young Children at School in the Inner City*, London: Erlbaum.

Wells, C.G. (1978) 'Talking with children: the complementary roles of parents and teachers', *English in Education* 12, 15–38.

Wells, G. (1986) *The Meaning Makers: Children Learning Language and Using Language to Learn*, Portsmouth: Heinemann Educational.

Young-Loveridge, J.M. (1987) 'Learning mathematics', *British Journal of Developmental Psychology* 5, 155–67.

Index